american bistro

dedication

For Michael and Laura, who make it all possible,

With love.

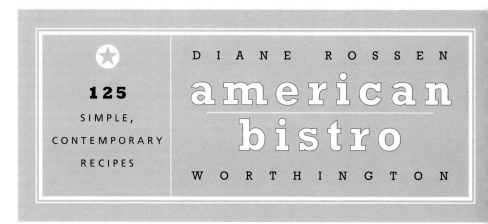

american bistro

DIANE ROSSEN WORTHINGTON

125 SIMPLE, CONTEMPORARY RECIPES

photographs by **JONELLE WEAVER**

CHRONICLE BOOKS

SAN FRANCISCO

A hardcover edition of this book was published in 1997
by Chronicle Books LLC.

Library of Congress Cataloging-in-Publication Data available.

ISBN 0-8118-3982-6

Manufactured in China.   —

INTERIOR
Food styling by Kimberly Huson
Prop styling by Anthony Albertus
Designed by Deborah Bowman

COVER
Baked Pork Chops Stuffed with Apples and Prunes, page 103.
Food styling by Liza Jernow
Prop styling by Paige Hicks
Designed by Brett MacFadden

Distributed in Canada by Raincoast Books
9050 Shaughnessy Street
Vancouver, BC V6P 6E5

10 9 8 7 6 5 4 3 2 1

Chronicle Books LLC
85 Second Street
San Francisco, California 94105

www.chroniclebooks.com

TABLE OF CONTENTS

acknowledgments ——

ETHAN ELLENBERG FOR PUTTING IT ALL TOGETHER AND ALWAYS COMING UP WITH INNOVATIVE IDEAS . BILL LEBLOND FOR BELIEVING IN THE PROJECT . LESLIE JONATH AND SHARON SILVA FOR HELPING ME TO FOCUS THE CONCEPT . SARAH PUTMAN FOR HER PATIENCE IN ANSWERING ALL MY QUESTIONS . JULIANNE TANTUM, AN ANGEL IN DISGUISE, FOR RECIPE DEVEL-OPMENT, TESTING, AND EDITING, AND WHOSE ENTHUSIASM, CREATIVITY, AND PRECISE ATTENTION TO THE SMALLEST DETAIL HELPED MAKE THIS BOOK ITS BEST . NYDIA OLIVARES FOR HER NEVER-ENDING SUPPORT ON THIS BOOK . KATHY BLUE FOR ALWAYS BEING AVAILABLE TO LOOK AT AN IDEA IN A DIFFERENT WAY AND FOR SOME OF THE MOST FUN COOKING DAYS EVER . ANDY BLUE FOR HIS INSIGHTFUL COMMENTARY ON PAIRING FOOD AND WINE AND HIS SPIRITED OPINIONS . DENNY LURIA, LAURIE BURROWS GRAD, CIJI WARE, CONNIE ENGEL, GINGER WORTHINGTON, JANICE WALD HENDERSON, JUDY MILLER, AND LUCY SUZAR FOR THEIR FRIENDSHIP . AND FINALLY, MY HUSBAND, MICHAEL, AND DAUGHTER, LAURA, FOR ALL THEIR SUPPORT.

Introduction

American Bistro was inspired by the European legacy of corner cafés. According to one story, the word *bistro* is derived from the Russian *bystro,* or "quickly," an order shouted by soldiers demanding faster service in Parisian cafés during the Russian occupation of France after the fall of Napoleon. By the mid-nineteenth century, France was the home of bistro cooking, as small, inexpensive restaurants turning out simply prepared dishes sprang up in great numbers in every city and town. Likewise in Italy, home-cooked favorites like pasta, pizza, and rotisseried poultry became standard fare in local trattorias.

Bistro-style cuisine in the United States today embraces both these European traditions and the casual simplicity of the American diner, adds another level of sophistication, and then translates it for the home cook. It is food defined by fresh ingredients, with a preference for locally grown, seasonal items. Most importantly, the American bistro marries the nation's longtime favorites with a growing passion for regional foods and ethnic flavors. It is a bold, unpretentious cuisine that has made its way onto menus of Napa Valley grills and New York cafés, Los Angeles bistros and Chicago trattorias.

Although much of my work over the years has been devoted to California cuisine, I have closely watched as bistro cooking has taken shape across America. Food that was once thought of as "home cooking" is being served up in neighborhood restaurants. Menus are becoming less complicated, offering the kind of comforting, straightforward dishes that belong to America's home kitchens. The result is a national table that is both rustic and sophisticated, earthy and eclectic. It is accessible food, a home-style meal served in a casual yet tasteful atmosphere that welcomes a range of diners, from symphony-bound couples to families with young children. And it is food that easily adapts to Americans' increasingly busy lifestyles, where meals must be quick and at the same time satisfying and delicious.

The following pages contain my personal definition of this contemporary cuisine, or what I call American bistro cooking. It is food that speaks to the soul and brings back a flood of memories, while simultaneously tying in new flavors and ingredients. If I were to open a restaurant today, this is the food I would serve: home cooking with a true American imprint.

American bistro food reflects our diversity as a nation and acknowledges our strong regional influences. From the Pacific Northwest we take smoked salmon for Belgian Endive Spears with Herbed Cream Cheese and Smoked Salmon, and plump blueberries and raspberries for Mixed Berry Bread Pudding. From the rich tapestry of the Southwest pantry comes Southwestern-style Beef Chili and Stir-fried Turkey and Vegetables with Avocado-Corn Salsa and Warm Corn Tortillas. And the waters of the Eastern seaboard bring Cornmeal-Crusted Soft-Shell Crabs with Lemon-Caper Sauce. At the center of these crossroads is America's heartland, where homemade sausages, wild game, and fresh cheeses are found in the Great Lakes region. The American bistro melds these national riches with European traditions to create the signature American cooking of today.

The recipes in this book capture the essence of the American bistro table through simple techniques such as grilling and roasting, and through the use of ethnic ingredients. Roasting vegetables intensifies their natural flavors and adds a sweet, caramelized taste to dishes such as Roasted Sweet Potato–Butternut Squash Soup with Herbed Sour Cream. Simple marinades tenderize and infuse meats with their flavors, as evidenced in Grilled Veal Chops with Fresh Thyme.

Those craving flavors that cross continental boundaries will find pleasure in an Asian-inspired Tuna Tartare with Cucumber-Avocado Relish, or the Eastern European Cabbage Beet Borscht. A variation on cool Indian yogurt *raitas* is the foundation of Grilled Citrus Chicken with Raita Sauce. An ancho chile livens up a seafood soup, Japanese bread crumbs add texture to crab cakes, and coconut milk enriches a tangy sauce for grilled shrimp. Ethnic foods have had a strong, steady influence on American bistro cooking, and they are rapidly finding their way onto supermarket shelves throughout the nation's cities and towns.

Today's home cooks can take advantage of the wonderful variety of quality gourmet products being produced throughout the country. Talented chefs are sharing their secrets by marketing flavored oils, vinegars, *demi-glace,* dried fruits, salsas, and specialty mustards. My recipes incorporate these innovations as time-savers for cooks with fast-paced lives. Basil-infused oil finishes off Whole Roasted Striped Bass on Sliced Potatoes, a touch of *demi-glace* enriches Roasted Rack of Lamb with

Herbed Crust, and sweetened dried cranberries add a unique accent to Chopped Winter Salad with Lemon-Mint Dressing.

American bistro cooking is built on traditional foods that reside in a culinary "comfort zone" that reflects our nostalgia for a host of past classics. Here, these familiar dishes appear in updated, highly appealing versions. For instance, a few contemporary ingredients modernize the beloved burger and dazzle the palate in Goat Cheese–Stuffed Hamburgers with Two-Olive Spread. The pot pie is given a new look and taste with the addition of leeks and cheese to become Chicken Pot Pie with Parmesan-Cheddar Crust, and lasagna loses its noodles but gains sophistication in Polenta Lasagna with Tomatoes and Peppers. Old-fashioned chocolate cake is elevated to Chocolate Celebration Cake, a fabulous-looking double-decker creation with chocolate chips and a whipped cream filling.

Exquisite fruits, organic vegetables, fresh herbs, and all kinds of game and fish continue to be cultivated and raised in America, and American bistro cooking celebrates that bounty. Weekly farmers' markets regularly turn up in downtown alleys, parking lots, ferry plazas, and parks in Los Angeles, New York, Chicago, San Francisco, New Orleans, Boston, and elsewhere. A visit to one of these markets delivers the freshest seasonal produce, a wide sampling of fruit varieties, a wealth of artisanal cheeses, and a gardenful of fresh herbs. Even home-delivery produce companies are sprouting up across the country, providing customers with weekly boxes of fruits and vegetables from nearby farms.

Today's focus on diet and fitness has prompted the development of lighter versions of old favorites. To this end, Pumpkin Caramel Flan previously made from whole evaporated milk works beautifully with low-fat evaporated milk. Golden Raisin–Bran Muffins turn out every bit as moist when applesauce is added in place of some of the oil.

Above all, American bistro cooking is adaptable. If tomatoes are not in season, go right ahead and use good-quality canned ones in recipes that call for cooking the tomatoes. If fresh baby peas are unavailable, feel free to use frozen. Make every attempt to use fresh herbs, but if certain herbs— thyme, oregano, rosemary, sage—cannot be found fresh, substitute the dried form, keeping in mind that you'll only need half the amount you use for fresh.

Inspired by an appreciation for the nation's most distinctive bistros, trattorias, and local grills, the following recipes promise that today's tastes can be happily passed on to the next generation.

a wine note

BY ANTHONY DIAS BLUE

The pairing of wine with food is an integral part of Western cuisine. It is one of the essential elements of how and what we eat. Tradition tells us, in no uncertain terms, "white with fish and fowl, red with meat and game." In the past, this rule was the foundation of wine and food interaction. Any deviation was considered unacceptable.

Times have changed, restaurants have changed, and so has the way we eat. Many of us dine at restaurants four or five times a week. The restaurant experience is not as "special" anymore; it's a normal, albeit pleasurable, part of our day. At home, and in restaurants, we eat simpler, more casual food. Instead of an appetizer, a fish course, a meat course, a cheese course, and dessert, we are likely to order only two dishes off a menu. Instead of several wines, we are likely to have just one.

Diane Worthington's *American Bistro* captures the essence of how we eat today. The food is hearty and flavorful, without being heavy or rich. It embraces concepts and combinations that stem from European bistros and trattorias, but it is unmistakably American in its ingredients and style. The wines that ideally accompany this food are the wines that American vintners make so well: hearty, full flavored, and unabashedly fruity and assertive.

Matching wines to America bistro food is easy. You can forget the long held rule and just wing it, keeping only a few uncomplicated guidelines in mind. Today's hot wines—buttery Chardonnays, crispy Sauvignon blancs, smoky Cabernets, luscious Merlots, lively Pinot Noirs, earthy Syrahs and fruity Zinfandels—are perfect with this kind of food.

The most important thing to look for is balance. Don't expect wines that are artfully subtle, or restrained and delicate, to stand up to this food. Save those for the tearoom. Match these dishes with wines that have a measure of brashness and assertiveness. Considerations of color—red wine, white wine—are less important. Surely, a crisp Sauvignon Blanc will be fine with Grilled Halibut with Eggplant-Olive Caponata (page 64), but a chilled Pinot Noir will be good, too. Cabernet with Roasted Rack of Lamb with Herbed Crust (page 102) is a perfect combination, but a big, rich Chardonnay won't be bad either.

The wines that fit the assertiveness description are—and here's good news—young and, by definition, relatively inexpensive. Keep your 1961 Château Margaux for a special occasion. Match these foods with wines that are still bursting with fruit and youthful enthusiasm.

And here's some more good news: beer is also a good match for this food. The current explosion of full-flavored micro brews is exceedingly well timed. Just when our food turned emphatic, so did our beer. A toasty stout goes nicely with Twice-Cooked Barbecued Chicken (page 75); a pale ale works well with Grilled Swordfish with Island Salsa (page 63). The hoppy, crisp flavors of beer are very much at home in the American bistro.

So the message is simple: use good sense and your own taste to select the beverages to go with this exciting, delicious American food. These are dishes with which to have fun. Why should the drink be any different?

Appetizers

tuna tartare with cucumber-avocado relish

One of the foundations of American bistro cooking is the art of bringing together ingredients from different cultures. This appetizer combines fresh tuna with a Japanese-and-Thai-inspired citrus–soy sauce dressing. The tuna is then topped with a refreshing cucumber-and-avocado mixture. Present the tartare elegantly, either in individual servings or as an opener for a cocktail party. Be sure to use only the freshest, top-quality raw tuna.

Dressing

2 garlic cloves, minced

1 teaspoon minced fresh ginger

1 teaspoon finely chopped fresh mint

2 tablespoons fresh orange juice

1 tablespoon fresh lime juice

2 teaspoons soy sauce

1½ teaspoons wasabi powder

2 teaspoons dark sesame oil

salt and freshly ground black pepper

Cucumber-Avocado Relish

1 medium cucumber

½ ripe avocado, pitted, peeled,
    and cut into ⅛-inch dice

3 tablespoons fresh lemon juice

1 teaspoon rice wine vinegar

salt and freshly ground black pepper

1 pound fresh tuna fillet, cut into
    ⅛-inch dice

Garnish

fresh mint leaves

1 baguette, cut into thin slices and
    lightly toasted

❶ Prepare the dressing: In a small bowl, whisk together all the dressing ingredients. Taste for seasoning. Cover and refrigerate until ready to serve the tartare. ❷ Prepare the relish: Peel the cucumber, cut in half lengthwise, and scoop out the seeds. Cut the cucumber into ⅛-inch dice. In a small bowl, stir together the cucumber, avocado, lemon juice, vinegar, salt, and pepper. Taste for seasoning. ❸ Place the tuna in a bowl. Add the dressing and mix gently, blending thoroughly. ❹ For individual servings, use a ⅓-cup measure to scoop out the tuna mixture and invert onto chilled plates. Surround the tuna with relish and scatter mint leaves on top of the relish. Place a few baguette slices on each plate. For a buffet, use a small bowl to shape the tuna into a single dome in the center of a serving plate. Surround with the relish, mint leaves, and baguette slices.

Advance Preparation: Can be prepared 2 hours ahead through step 2, covered, and refrigerated.

[SERVES 6]

whitefish terrine with beet-horseradish relish

The ground whitefish used here is the same fish used for the popular Jewish dish gefilte fish, and is regularly available in many supermarkets and fish markets during Jewish holidays. If you can't find the fish ground, process the fillets in the food processor, making sure first to remove the skin and all the bones. (You'll need about 2 pounds whitefish fillets with the skin on if you are going to grind it yourself.) The accompanying bright red beet-horseradish relish adds a burst of color and flavor to the chilled terrine. This terrine can be served in overlapping slices either on individual plates or on a large platter with crisp crackers, matzo or thinly sliced pumpernickel bread. Pass the colorful relish separately.

❶ In a skillet, heat the oil over medium heat. Add the carrots and onion and sauté for 5 to 7 minutes, or until softened. Remove from the heat and let cool for 10 minutes. ❷ Preheat the oven to 350 degrees F. Lightly coat a 9-by-5-by-2½-inch loaf pan with nonstick cooking spray. ❸ In a large bowl, with an electric mixer set on medium speed, beat the eggs with the matzo meal. When well combined, add the stock, fish, cooled carrots and onion, salt, pepper, and sugar and continue to beat until well blended. ❹ Pour the mixture into the prepared pan. Pick up the pan with both hands and slam it down on the counter to settle any air bubbles. Drizzle the lime juice over the top and sprinkle with the paprika. Bake for 50 to 60 minutes, or until a long wooden skewer inserted into the center comes out clean. ❺ Meanwhile, prepare the relish. Place the horseradish cream and roasted beets in a food processor fitted with the metal blade and process until puréed. Transfer to a small container, cover, and refrigerate. ❻ Remove the terrine from oven and let cool for 15 minutes. Cover with aluminum foil and chill overnight. ❼ Loosen the sides of the terrine from the pan by running a knife blade along the edges. Invert the terrine onto a plate, then turn upright on a platter. Slice, garnish with lemon slices and parsley, and serve. Pass the Beet-Horseradish Relish separately.

Advance Preparation: Can be prepared up to 2 days ahead, covered, and refrigerated.

[SERVES 10 ➡ 12]

2 tablespoons olive oil

3 carrots, peeled and finely chopped

1 large onion, finely chopped

3 large eggs

3½ tablespoons matzo meal

¾ cup chicken stock, fish stock, or water

1½ pounds ground whitefish or a mixture
    of whitefish, pike, and buffalo fish

2 teaspoons salt

¾ teaspoon white pepper

½ teaspoon sugar

1 tablespoon fresh lime juice

¼ teaspoon paprika

1 jar (5 ounces) prepared horseradish cream

2 Basic Roasted Beets (page 178)

Garnish

lemon slices

parsley sprigs

belgian endive spears with herbed
cream cheese and smoked salmon

In the 1980s, the production of such European pantry staples as radicchio, exotic mushrooms, goat cheese, and olive oil became American cottage industries. Even Belgian endive is now grown in California, and a red variety as well as the more common white variety are cultivated.

When purchasing Belgian endives, look for large stalks that are creamy white, shading to pale yellow at the tips. Since endives are grown from roots that are "forced" to bud in dark growing rooms, they never touch dirt and therefore do not need to be washed. Assemble these colorful spears at the last minute as light causes the leaves to change color. I like to serve them at a formal dinner party or a cocktail party.

❶ Prepare the salsa: Combine all the ingredients in a small bowl and stir to mix well. Taste for seasoning. Drain off excess liquid, cover, and set aside. ❷ In a food processor fitted with the metal blade, combine the cream cheese and dill and process until the cream cheese is whipped slightly and the dill is evenly blended. ❸ Separate the endive spears (as you get closer to the center, you may have to trim the bottom of the head to free the spears). ❹ Spoon the cream cheese mixture into a large plastic bag, pushing it down to one corner. Cut off about ¼ inch from the filled corner tip of the bag, or a piece just wide enough to push the cream cheese through. Pipe some herbed cream cheese onto the blunt end of each Belgian endive spear. (Alternatively, you can use a teaspoon to spread the cream cheese onto the endive spears.) Place some of the chopped salmon on top, then spoon about 1 teaspoon of the salsa onto the salmon. ❺ To serve, arrange the spears on a serving platter and garnish with parsley sprigs.

Advance Preparation: Can be prepared up to 1 day ahead through step 2, covered, and refrigerated. Bring to room temperature before continuing.

[SERVES 6]

Salsa

1 small red tomato, seeded and finely diced

1 small yellow tomato, seeded and finely diced

3 scallions, white and light green parts only, finely chopped

salt and freshly ground black pepper

4 ounces cream cheese, at room temperature

2 tablespoons finely chopped fresh dill

2 large heads Belgian endive

1½ ounces smoked salmon, finely chopped

parsley sprigs, for garnish

smoked fish mousse

Guests always rave when I serve this appetizer, which also happens to be incredibly quick to prepare. Search out a good-quality smoked fish from a reliable purveyor at a specialty fish market or deli. The fish should be lightly smoked to create a subtle balance of flavors. Prepare the mousse a day ahead of serving to allow time for the flavors to mellow and blend, and adjust the seasoning to taste based on the type of fish used.

1 shallot

½ pound lean smoked trout or whitefish,
*   all skin and bones removed*

6 tablespoons mayonnaise

3 tablespoons cream cheese,
*   room temperature*

1½ tablespoons fresh lime juice

1 tablespoon finely chopped fresh dill

white pepper

fresh dill sprigs, for garnish

lightly toasted thin baguette slices

❶ In a food processor fitted with the metal blade, mince the shallot. Add the fish, mayonnaise, cream cheese, lime juice, chopped dill, and white pepper, and process until puréed. Taste for seasoning. ❷ Spoon the mousse into a 1½-cup crock and garnish with dill sprigs. Serve with baguette slices.

Advance Preparation: Can be prepared up to 3 days ahead, covered, and refrigerated. Garnish just before serving.

MAKES 1 CUP [SERVES 4 ➡ 6]

bistro pâté with cornichons, olives, and assorted mustards

This bistro-style pâté breaks with tradition. It uses turkey instead of pork, while pistachio nuts and chopped ham give it a rustic look. The recipe makes enough pâté to fill one standard loaf pan and a small loaf pan, the latter an ideal size to give away as a gift.

Caul fat, a thin, fatty membrane from pig or sheep, is used to wrap pâtés. It resembles a lacy net and melts away as the pâté cooks. If necessary, soak the caul fat in warm salted water before using to loosen the layers and prevent tearing. If you can't find caul or back fat (thinly sliced pieces of pork fat), long strips of bacon with ample fat can be substituted. This is an ideal starter before Grilled Seafood Soup with Ancho Chile Rouille (page 40). It's also excellent for picnics.

❶ Preheat the oven to 300 degrees F. In a large mixing bowl, combine the veal, turkey, pork fat, ham, brandy, shallots, and flour and mix well. Add the eggs, cream, parsley, chicken livers, salt, and pepper, and mix well again. Add the oregano, thyme, allspice, cinnamon, nutmeg, and pistachio nuts, and stir to distribute evenly. ❷ Line a 9-by-5-by-2½-inch loaf pan and a 6-by-3½-by 2½-inch loaf pan with the caul fat or back fat, making sure that the interiors of the pans are completely covered and that the fat hangs a couple of inches over the edges. Spoon the meat mixture into the pans, patting it down into the corners so there are no air bubbles. Cover with the overhanging fat and place a bay leaf in the center of each pâté. Cover them with aluminum foil. ❸ Place each loaf pan in a larger baking pan. Add enough almost-boiling water to the baking pans to come halfway up the sides of the loaf pans. Bake the small loaf for 2½ hours and the large loaf for 3½ hours. ❹ Remove the baking pans from the oven and remove the loaf pans. Let cool on a rack. When cool, drain off the fat and invert the pâtés onto a work surface or platter. Blot off all the excess fat. Wrap each pâté in aluminum foil and place them on a baking sheet. Place a brick or other weight on top of each pâté to press it down for at least 12 hours. Refrigerate for at least 1 day, or for up to 5 days. ❺ To serve, cut into ½-inch-thick slices and present on individual plates. Garnish each plate with parsley sprigs, cornichons, and baguette slices. Pass the mustards at the table.

Advance Preparation: Can be prepared up to 5 days ahead, covered, and refrigerated. Remove from the refrigerator 1 hour before serving.

[SERVES 8 ➡ 10]

1 pound veal stew meat, ground

1 pound turkey meat, ground

½ pound pork fat, ground

1 cup cooked ham, cut into small pieces

½ cup Cognac or other brandy

4 shallots, finely chopped

¼ cup all-purpose flour

2 large eggs

⅓ cup whipping cream

½ cup finely chopped parsley

¼ pound chicken livers, ground

salt and freshly ground black pepper

1 teaspoon finely chopped fresh oregano
    or ½ teaspoon dried

1 teaspoon finely chopped fresh thyme
    or ½ teaspoon dried

½ teaspoon ground allspice

½ teaspoon ground cinnamon

¼ teaspoon freshly grated nutmeg

¼ cup pistachio nuts

¾ pound caul fat or thinly sliced back fat

2 bay leaves

Garnish

parsley sprigs

cornichons

thin baguette slices

assorted mustards such as Dijon and grainy

two-olive spread

California orchards are becoming home to rows of European olive trees, spurring the creation of interesting adaptations of traditional olive pastes. This colorful spread, a variation on Provençal tapenade, combines black and green olives. In this recipe, you can use any California or European green olive that blends well with the rich, salty black Kalamatas of Greece. Rinse the olives well if they have been packed in a particularly strong brine. Use this spread on crackers or Parmesan Crisps (page 26) as appetizers, or add it to a vinaigrette or tomato-based sauce to perk up the flavors.

20 Kalamata olives, pitted, rinsed,
    and drained
20 green olives, pitted, rinsed, and drained
½ Peeled Red Bell Pepper
    (page 177), chopped
1 tablespoon capers, rinsed and drained
2 tablespoons finely chopped Italian parsley
⅛ teaspoon cayenne pepper
3 tablespoons olive oil

❶ In a food processor fitted with the metal blade, combine the olives, chopped pepper, capers, parsley, and cayenne pepper and process until coarsely chopped. Then use on-off pulses while slowly adding the olive oil until it is absorbed. Taste for seasoning. Transfer to an airtight container and refrigerate until ready to use.

Advance Preparation: Can be prepared up to 1 week ahead, covered, and refrigerated.

MAKES 1 CUP [SERVES 4 ➡ 6]

roasted eggplant–garlic spread

This eggplant spread sparkles with Mediterranean ingredients. Roasting the garlic adds a nutty, sweet flavor, while sautéing and glazing the onions in balsamic vinegar contributes a touch of caramel flavor. Salting and roasting the eggplant reduces the moisture that accumulates when eggplants are cooked whole, resulting in a spread with a deliciously thick texture. Try this on Crispy Pizza Toasts (page 29) or Parmesan Crisps (page 26), or on any grilled breads or toasts. It is also wonderful with Herbed Garlic Cheese Bread (page 27).

❶ Peel the eggplant and cut crosswise into ½-inch-thick slices. Place in a colander, sprinkle with the coarse salt, weight down with a plate, and let drain for about 20 minutes. Rinse and pat dry. While the eggplant slices are weighted, preheat the oven to 400 degrees F. ❷ Brush the eggplant slices lightly on both sides with 1 teaspoon of the olive oil and place on a baking sheet. Wrap the garlic cloves in a piece of aluminum foil and place on the baking sheet. Bake for 10 minutes, then flip the eggplant slices and continue to bake for 15 more minutes or until tender. Remove the baking sheet from the oven, let the eggplant cool, and chop coarsely. Set the garlic aside. ❸ Meanwhile, heat the remaining 1 tablespoon olive oil in a small skillet over medium-high heat. Add the onion and sauté for 6 to 8 minutes, or until softened. Add the vinegar and reduce while sautéing for another 2 minutes. ❹ In a food processor fitted with the metal blade, combine the eggplant, onion mixture, lemon juice, basil, and Parmesan, and process until puréed. Using your fingers, squeeze the garlic pulp into the processor and process until blended. Add salt and pepper and taste for seasoning. Transfer to an airtight container and refrigerate until ready to use.

Advance Preparation: Can be prepared up to 3 days ahead, covered, and refrigerated.

MAKES 1 CUP [SERVES 4 ➡ 6]

1 small eggplant

1 teaspoon coarse salt

1 tablespoon plus 1 teaspoon olive oil

2 garlic cloves, unpeeled

1 onion, finely chopped

2 teaspoons balsamic vinegar

1 tablespoon fresh lemon juice

1 tablespoon finely chopped fresh basil

1 tablespoon freshly grated Parmesan cheese

salt and freshly ground black pepper

baked artichokes with
bread crumbs, tomatoes, and parmesan

California provides nearly all of the nation's commercial artichokes, with most of them coming from Monterey County on the central coast. The sandy soil and cool, fog-shrouded days lured Italian immigrants to plant this edible thistle in the 1880s, and row after row have been thriving there ever since.

To preserve the shape of the artichokes, bake them whole with an Italian-influenced mixture of bread crumbs, tomatoes, garlic, herbs, and Parmesan cheese stuffed between the layers of leaves. As you pull off the leaves, you taste both the artichoke and the complementary stuffing. This dish is hearty enough to serve as a vegetarian main course along with Roasted Butternut Squash–Sweet Potato Soup with Herbed Sour Cream (page 37).

4 large artichokes

2 tablespoons distilled white vinegar

1 teaspoon olive oil

Filling

3 tomatoes, peeled, seeded, and finely diced

4 garlic cloves, minced

3 tablespoons finely chopped fresh basil

3 tablespoons finely chopped parsley

3 tablespoons olive oil

3 cups coarse fresh French bread crumbs

*½ cup plus 2 tablespoons freshly grated
    Parmesan cheese*

salt and freshly ground black pepper

½ cup chicken stock

Advance Preparation: Can be prepared up to 8 hours ahead through step 3, covered, and refrigerated. Bring to room temperature before continuing.

[SERVES 4]

❶ Using a serrated knife, and working with 1 artichoke at a time, slice off about ½ inch of the top of the artichoke to remove the main cluster of thorns. Trim the stems flush with the bottoms. Pull off the small, tough leaves from the bottom and discard. Using sharp scissors, cut ½ inch off the top of the outer leaves to remove the thorny tips. ❷ Fill a large pan half-full of water, and add the vinegar and 1 teaspoon olive oil. Cover the pan and bring the water to a boil over high heat. Add the artichokes, re-cover, and simmer for 40 to 50 minutes, or until the bottoms (where the stems were) can be pierced easily with a knife. (If you have used smaller artichokes, they will cook a bit faster.) ❸ Using tongs, remove the artichokes from the pan and place them on a rack, stem ends up, to drain as they cool. ❹ Meanwhile, prepare the filling: In a bowl, combine the tomatoes, garlic, basil, parsley, and 1 tablespoon of the olive oil. Stir and toss to mix. Stir in the bread crumbs, distributing them evenly. Mix in the Parmesan cheese, salt, and pepper. Taste for seasoning. ❺ Preheat the oven to 425 degrees F. When the artichokes are cool, turn them upright on their stems and, working from the center, gently pull open the leaves to reveal the sharp-tipped inner leaves. Using your fingers, pull out the prickly leaves and discard. Using a teaspoon, scrape out and discard the fuzzy center covering each bottom. ❻ Spoon some of the filling into the center cavity of each artichoke, then spoon the remaining filling in between the rows of leaves. ❼ Arrange the stuffed artichokes in a baking dish. In a small bowl, stir together the stock and the remaining 2 tablespoons olive oil. Drizzle over the tops of the artichokes. Bake for 10 to 15 minutes, or until the stuffing turns golden. Watch to make sure the tips of the artichoke leaves don't get too brown. ❽ To serve, place the warm or room-temperature artichokes on a serving platter or individual plates.

parmesan crisps

These small toasts create a crispy backdrop for a variety of savory spreads, such as Two-Olive Spread (page 22) and Roasted Eggplant–Garlic Spread (page 23). Their flavor also makes them great croutons for crumbling over a simple salad or dunking into a favorite vegetable soup. You can try other cheeses as well, such as dry Sonoma Jack or pecorino, just as long as they are full flavored.

*24 thin slices French or sourdough
    baguette (about 2½ inches in diameter)*
2 tablespoons unsalted butter, melted
2 tablespoons olive oil
⅓ cup freshly grated Parmesan cheese

❶ Preheat the oven to 375 degrees F. Place the bread slices on a baking sheet and toast for 5 minutes, or until dry and firm but not golden. ❷ Meanwhile, in a small bowl, combine the melted butter and olive oil and stir to mix well. Place the Parmesan on a flat plate. When the bread slices are ready, remove from the oven and brush each toast on both sides with some of the butter mixture and then press each slice into the cheese to coat evenly on both sides. Return the toasts to the baking sheet and bake for 5 to 7 minutes, or until the cheese is melted but not browned. Watch carefully, as they burn easily. Let cool and serve.

Advance Preparation: Can be prepared up to 3 days ahead and stored in an airtight container at room temperature.

MAKES 24 TOASTS [SERVES 4 ➡ 6]

herbed garlic cheese bread

This sophisticated version of the old American standby is every bit as good served with a glass of wine or with a hearty pasta. Combining olive oil with butter decreases the richness without sacrificing flavor. Loaves of crusty French bread are first spread with an herbed butter–olive oil compound and then wrapped in aluminum foil. While the bread bakes, the Parmesan cheese–olive oil blend infuses it to create an irresistibly aromatic starter for any barbecue or summer dinner. Unwrapping the foil for the last 5 minutes browns the top slightly and adds a bit of crispiness to the bread.

❶ In a small bowl, combine the butter, olive oil, and mustard, and mix until well blended. Add the garlic, ¼ cup of the Parmesan cheese, the basil, thyme, oregano, salt, and pepper. Mix well. ❷ Preheat the oven to 400 degrees F. Slice the bread in half lengthwise. Spread each cut side with half of the herbed butter mixture. Sprinkle the halves with the remaining ¼ cup Parmesan cheese. ❸ Cut each bread half vertically into 2-inch-wide slices, cutting only three-fourths of the way through. (By not cutting all the way through, the bread will still hold together). Wrap each of the bread halves in aluminum foil and close the ends tightly. ❹ Place the wrapped halves on a baking sheet and bake for 10 minutes. Remove the foil, return the halves to the oven, and bake for another 5 minutes, or until the top is golden and the bread is crisp. Serve immediately.

Advance Preparation: Can be prepared up to 4 hours ahead through step 3, covered, and refrigerated. Remove from the refrigerator 30 minutes before baking.

[SERVES 8]

¼ cup unsalted butter, room temperature

¼ cup olive oil

1 teaspoon grainy mustard

3 garlic cloves, minced

½ cup freshly grated Parmesan cheese

1 tablespoon finely chopped fresh basil

½ teaspoon finely chopped fresh thyme

⅛ teaspoon finely chopped fresh oregano
　　or pinch of dried

salt and white pepper

1 large loaf French or sourdough bread

griddled quesadillas with
caramelized fennel and red onions

The quesadilla, a traditional Mexican appetizer, can be simple fare with a plain melted-cheese center (which kids love) or an elaborate turnover. In either case, a flour tortilla is filled, folded over, and lightly fried or baked to brown the outside and heat the filling. Here, slightly sweet-and-sour Caramelized Fennel and Red Onions become the filling. You'll have some filling left over, which is delicious as a spread, tucked into omelets, or served as a relish alongside grilled sausages. For a spicier twist, toss a jalapeño chile in with the fennel and onions. You can also experiment with different Mexican cheeses.

nonstick cooking spray or vegetable oil
3 flour tortillas, each 12 inches in diameter
1 ½ cups Caramelized Fennel
and Red Onions (page 185)
1 ½ cups shredded Monterey Jack cheese

Garnish
1 tablespoon finely chopped parsley
½ cup Tomatillo Salsa (page 183)
½ cup sour cream

❶ Lightly spray a 12-inch nonstick skillet or griddle with nonstick cooking spray or add 1 tablespoon vegetable oil. Place over medium-high heat for 1 minute. Place a tortilla in the skillet and spoon ½ cup of the fennel-onion mixture evenly over one-half. Sprinkle with ½ cup of the cheese, and fold the tortilla in half, pressing it down with a spatula. ❷ Cook the quesadilla for 2 to 3 minutes, or until lightly browned, then turn it over and cook the other side until lightly browned. Place on a cutting board, slice into wedges, and keep warm under aluminum foil. ❸ Repeat the process with the remaining tortillas and filling. Arrange the wedges on a large serving platter and garnish with the parsley. Serve immediately accompanied with salsa and sour cream.

Advance Preparation: Caramelized Fennel and Red Onions can be prepared up to 3 days ahead, covered, and refrigerated. Remove from the refrigerator 1 hour before continuing.

[SERVES 6]

crispy pizza toasts

Serve these intensely flavored little toasts alone or with soups or salads. The sun-dried tomato pesto gives the toasts an extra bite of rich tomato flavor. You can easily double or triple this recipe for a large party.

❶ Preheat the oven to 375 degrees F. Place the bread slices on a baking sheet and toast them for 5 minutes, or until dry and firm but not golden. ❷ In a small bowl, combine the olive oil and Sun-Dried Tomato Pesto and stir to mix well. Brush each toast with some of the mixture. Sprinkle evenly with the Parmesan. ❸ Return the toasts to the oven and bake for about 5 more minutes or until the cheese is melted but not browned. Watch carefully, as they burn easily. Let cool and serve.

Advance Preparation: Can be prepared up to 3 days ahead and stored in an airtight container at room temperature.

MAKES 24 TOASTS [SERVES 4 ➡ 6]

*24 thin slices French or sourdough baguette
    (about 2½ inches in diameter)*
2 tablespoons plus 1 teaspoon olive oil
¼ cup Sun-Dried Tomato Pesto (page 180)
3 tablespoons freshly grated Parmesan cheese

Soups and Salads

white bean soup with tomatoes and spinach

The beans take on a creamy consistency when cooked, resulting in a velvety texture without the addition of cream. Wilted spinach leaves stirred in just before serving impart a vibrant green accent to the finished soup. If you don't have white beans, dried lima beans can be substituted. I like to serve this soup for lunch on a cool autumn day with Quinoa and Cracked Wheat Vegetable Salad (page 56).

2 cups dried white beans such as Great
    Northern
2 tablespoons olive oil
2 large onions, finely chopped
2 carrots, peeled and thinly sliced
2 tomatoes, peeled, seeded, and finely
    chopped
3 garlic cloves, minced
8 cups chicken stock
salt and freshly ground black pepper
¼ cup finely chopped parsley
2 tablespoons balsamic vinegar
pinch of cayenne pepper
1 bunch spinach, cleaned, stemmed, and
    coarsely shredded

Garnish

1 tomato, peeled, seeded, and finely diced
¼ cup finely chopped mixed fresh herbs,
    such as chives, thyme, and parsley
¼ cup freshly grated Parmesan cheese

❶ Soak the beans overnight in cold water to cover generously. Or use a quick-soak method: Bring the beans to a boil in water to cover, boil for 2 minutes, remove from the heat, and let stand for 1 hour. Drain the beans and set aside. ❷ In a 6-quart soup pot, heat the olive oil over medium heat. Add the onions and sauté, stirring occasionally, for about 5 minutes, or until soft. Add the carrots and tomatoes and sauté for another 3 minutes. Add the garlic, and sauté for 1 minute longer. Add the chicken stock, beans, salt, and pepper. Bring to a simmer, cover partially, and cook for about 1 hour, or until the beans are tender. ❸ Purée the soup until smooth in the pan with a hand blender or in batches in a food processor fitted with the metal blade. Pass the soup through a fine-meshed strainer into a large saucepan. ❹ Reheat the soup over medium heat. Add the parsley, vinegar, cayenne pepper, and spinach. Cook for 2 to 3 minutes, or until the spinach is cooked but still bright green. Taste for seasoning. ❺ Ladle into soup bowls. Garnish the soup with the tomato, herbs, and Parmesan cheese, and serve immediately.

Advance Preparation: Can be prepared up to 3 days ahead through step 3, covered, and refrigerated. Reheat gently. This soup also freezes well for up to 1 month. Adjust the seasonings when you reheat the frozen soup.

·[SERVES 6 ➡ 8]

cabbage beet borscht

Borscht is often thought of as a Russian soup, but through the years it has made its way onto many American deli menus. This dressed-up version uses only vegetables, which makes it decidedly lighter than its beef-based cousin. The leeks, carrots, cabbage, and beets are first oven-roasted to bring out their rich flavors. Puréeing some of the roasted beets turns the soup an appealing garnet red. You can substitute light sour cream for the dilled cream, or simply garnish with a sprig of dill. Serve this satisfying cold-weather meal with warm French bread. This is a great dish for a crowd.

❶ Preheat the oven to 425 degrees F. In a large roasting pan, combine the olive oil, leeks, carrots and garlic and mix with a large spoon to coat all the ingredients evenly with the oil. Place in the oven and roast for 15 minutes. Using long oven mitts to protect your hands, stir the vegetables, add the cabbage, and mix well to combine. Continue to roast for 10 minutes longer or until nicely browned. ❷ Meanwhile, place half of the roasted beets and the ¼ cup beet liquid in the bowl of a food processor fitted with the metal blade and process to purée. Reserve the beet purée. Cut the remaining beets into ½-inch dice and reserve. ❸ Place the potatoes in a saucepan. Add 4 cups of the chicken stock, and bring to a boil over medium-high heat. Cook for about 10 minutes, or until tender. Remove from the heat and reserve the potatoes and their cooking liquid. ❹ Remove the roasted vegetables from the oven and transfer to a large dutch oven, making sure to scrape all the browned bits from the bottom of the roasting pan into the pot. Add the puréed beets, tomato paste, dill, vinegar, brown sugar, the remaining 2 cups chicken stock, salt, and pepper. Bring to a simmer over medium-high heat, stirring until the sugar dissolves, for about 3 minutes. ❺ Add the reserved diced beets, the potatoes, and 3 cups of the potato cooking liquid. Return to a simmer and cook for 15 minutes. Taste for seasoning. ❻ Prepare the Dilled Cream: In a small bowl, stir together all the ingredients. Taste for seasoning. ❼ To serve, ladle the borscht into deep soup bowls and garnish with the Dilled Cream and a sprig of dill.

Advance Preparation: Can be prepared up to 3 days ahead, covered, and refrigerated. Reheat gently and adjust the seasonings.

[SERVES 8 ➡ 10]

2 tablespoons olive oil

2 leeks, white and light green parts only, cleaned and finely chopped

2 carrots, peeled and coarsely chopped

3 garlic cloves, halved

1 head green cabbage, coarsely shredded

6 Basic Roasted Beets (page 178), including ¼ cup of the beet liquid

8 red new potatoes, cut in half

6 cups chicken stock

2 tablespoons tomato paste

1½ teaspoons finely chopped fresh dill or ¾ teaspoon dried

5 tablespoons balsamic vinegar or red wine vinegar

⅓ cup plus 1 tablespoon lightly packed brown sugar

salt and freshly ground black pepper

Dilled Cream

½ cup sour cream

2 tablespoons finely chopped fresh dill

2 teaspoons fresh lemon juice

salt

fresh dill sprigs, for garnish

tomato bisque

Bisques are often thought of as creamy shellfish soups thickened with rice or potatoes. Vegetable soups puréed to create a creamy consistency are sometimes recognized as bisques as well. This recipe makes a point of incorporating the tomato skins as part of the texture of the soup, so be sure to seed the tomatoes, but don't bother peeling them.

There are many variations on this comforting dish. If you prefer a richer soup, you can substitute half-and-half or whipping cream for the milk. If you want a smooth texture, pass the soup through a strainer. If you like the flavor of fresh herbs, add chopped fresh chives, fresh basil, or even mint to the soup while it cooks, and sprinkle it with the same herb just before serving. For a satisfying lunch, serve the bisque with Parmesan Crisps (page 26) and Country Chicken Salad Niçoise (page 45).

¼ cup olive oil

1 onion, thinly sliced

1 carrot, peeled and finely chopped

1 stalk celery, finely chopped

1 garlic clove, minced

¼ cup all-purpose flour

6 ripe tomatoes, seeded and
    coarsely chopped

¼ cup tomato paste

½ teaspoon sugar

2¼ cups chicken stock

1½ cups milk

salt and white pepper

12 Parmesan Crisps (page 26) or ½ cup
    cheese or garlic croutons, for garnish

❶ In a large, heavy saucepan, heat the olive oil over medium heat. Add the onion and sauté for 3 to 4 minutes, or until softened. Add the carrot and celery and sauté for 4 to 5 minutes longer, or until they begin to soften. Add the garlic and sauté for 1 minute, or until slightly softened. ❷ Sprinkle the flour over the vegetables and continue to cook over low heat, stirring constantly, for 1 to 2 minutes, or until the flour is incorporated into the vegetables and has thickened. Add the tomatoes, tomato paste, sugar, and chicken stock, increase the heat to medium-high, and bring to a simmer. ❸ Cover partially, reduce the heat to medium, and cook, stirring occasionally, for 20 minutes, or until the vegetables are tender and all the flavors are well blended. ❹ Purée the soup in the pan with a hand blender or in batches in a blender, making sure to leave a little texture. Return the soup to the pan if necessary. ❺ Add the milk, and salt and pepper to taste and reheat over medium heat, stirring to combine. Taste for seasoning. ❻ To serve, ladle the soup into bowls and garnish with the Parmesan Crisps or a few croutons just before serving.

Advance Preparation: Can be prepared up to 1 day ahead through step 5, covered, and refrigerated. Reheat gently and adjust the seasonings.

[SERVES 4 ➡ 6]

lima bean soup with sun-dried tomato cream

Native Americans popularized the lima bean by cooking it with fresh sweet corn, calling the resulting mixture *msickquatash* (succotash). The stew became a popular colonial dish, and is still found on dinner tables across the country. Lima beans, sometimes called butter beans or pole beans, are showcased here in a smooth, bright green soup that combines zucchini and peas with the creamy lima bean. A dollop of tomato cream swirled into the finished soup adds a contemporary colorful touch.

❶ In a large saucepan or dutch oven, heat the olive oil over medium-high heat. Add the onions and zucchini and sauté, stirring often, for 5 to 7 minutes, or until just golden. ❷ Add the chicken stock and return to a boil. Add the lima beans and peas. When the soup returns to a boil, reduce the heat to medium and simmer for 20 to 25 minutes, or until the vegetables are softened. Add the salt and pepper. ❸ Purée the soup until completely smooth in the pan with a hand blender or in batches in a blender or a food processor fitted with the metal blade. Return the soup to the pan if necessary. Reheat over medium heat. Taste for seasoning. ❹ Meanwhile, prepare the Tomato Cream: In a small bowl, stir together the tomato pesto and sour cream to form a smooth, pale red mixture. ❺ To serve, ladle into bowls and swirl a spoonful of the tomato cream into each bowl.

Advance Preparation: Can be prepared up to 2 days ahead through step 4, covered, and refrigerated. Reheat gently. This soup also freezes well for up to 1 month. Adjust the seasonings when you reheat the frozen soup.

[SERVES 6]

2 tablespoons olive oil

2 onions, thinly sliced

4 zucchini, thinly sliced

4 cups chicken stock

2 cups fresh or frozen, small or large
      lima beans

1 cup fresh or frozen peas

salt and freshly ground black pepper

Sun-Dried Tomato Cream

¼ cup Sun-Dried Tomato Pesto (page 180)

¼ cup sour cream or nonfat plain yogurt

roasted butternut squash–sweet potato soup with herbed sour cream

In this recipe, it is important to select the moist, reddish brown–skinned sweet potatoes (often labeled yams), rather than the drier, yellowish-skinned sweet potatoes, which are far less sweet. Swirling in a dollop of herb-laced sour cream enhances the flavor and texture of this smooth orange soup without adding lots of fat. This makes a wonderful lunch when paired with American Bistro Caesar Salad with Roasted Garlic Dressing (page 50).

❶ Preheat the oven to 425 degrees F. In a large bowl, combine the sweet potatoes, squash, onion, thyme, and sage. Add the olive oil and toss to coat all the vegetables evenly with the oil. Spoon the mixture onto a large baking sheet, spreading out the vegetables in a single layer. ❷ Roast the vegetables, stirring twice, for 35 to 40 minutes, or until caramelized. Use long oven mitts to protect your hands when stirring. ❸ Remove from the oven and place half of the vegetables in a food processor fitted with the metal blade. Add 2 cups of the chicken stock and process until smooth. Place in a large saucepan and repeat with remaining vegetables and 2 cups of the stock. ❹ Add the remaining 1 cup stock, the nutmeg, salt, and pepper to the soup, and bring to a simmer over medium heat. Taste for seasoning. ❺ Meanwhile, prepare the Herbed Sour Cream: In a small bowl, stir together all the ingredients. Taste for seasoning. ❻ To serve, ladle the soup into bowls. Swirl a spoonful of the Herbed Sour Cream into each bowl and sprinkle with the thyme. Serve immediately.

Advance Preparation: Can be prepared up to 1 day ahead through step 5, covered, and refrigerated. Reheat gently. This soup also freezes well for up to 1 month. Adjust the seasonings when you reheat the frozen soup.

[SERVES 6]

2 pounds reddish brown–skinned sweet
    potatoes (about 3 medium),
    peeled and cut into 1-inch pieces
    (see recipe introduction)
1 small butternut squash, about
    1¼ pounds, halved, seeded, peeled,
    and cut into 1-inch pieces
1 onion, quartered
1 tablespoon finely chopped fresh thyme
1 tablespoon finely chopped fresh sage
1½ tablespoons olive oil
5 cups chicken stock
pinch of freshly grated nutmeg
salt and white pepper

Herbed Sour Cream
½ cup sour cream
1 teaspoon finely chopped fresh thyme
1 teaspoon finely chopped fresh sage
salt and white pepper

finely chopped fresh thyme, for garnish

purée of vegetable soup with pesto swirl

For an earthier flavor, add a cup of cooked garbanzo beans to the soup before puréeing. I like to serve each bowl with a swirl of pesto for a pretty contrast of flavors and colors. You can vary this soup with other vegetables, but don't forget to include the parsnip for its distinctive flavor.

2 tablespoons olive oil

3 leeks, white and light green parts only, cleaned and finely chopped

2 garlic cloves, minced

4 carrots, peeled and cut into 2-inch pieces

2 parsnips, peeled and cut into 2-inch pieces

4 zucchini, cut into 2-inch pieces

3 white potatoes, peeled and cut into 2-inch pieces

2 tablespoons tomato paste

8 cups chicken stock

2 tablespoons finely chopped parsley

2 tablespoons finely chopped fresh thyme

salt and freshly ground black pepper

2 tablespoons fresh lemon juice

½ cup Basic Pesto (page 179)

2 tablespoons finely chopped parsley, for garnish

❶ In a large saucepan or Dutch oven, heat the olive oil over medium-high heat. Add leeks and sauté for 3 to 5 minutes, or until softened. Add the garlic and sauté for 1 minute longer. Add the carrots, parsnips, zucchini, potatoes, tomato paste, 7 cups of the stock, 1 tablespoon of the parsley, 1 tablespoon of the thyme, salt, and pepper. Mix together well. Cover partially and simmer over medium heat for 30 to 35 minutes, or until the potatoes are tender. ❷ Purée the soup until smooth in the pan with a hand blender or in batches in a food processor fitted with the metal blade. Return the soup to the pan if necessary. Add the remaining 1 cup stock and bring to a simmer over medium heat. Add the remaining 1 tablespoon each parsley and thyme and the lemon juice, and cook for 3 minutes. Taste for seasoning. ❸ To serve, ladle the soup into warmed bowls. Swirl in a tablespoon of pesto and garnish with the parsley.

Advance Preparation: Can be prepared up to 3 days in advance, covered, and refrigerated. Reheat gently and adjust the seasonings.

[SERVES 8]

mushroom barley soup

Try this hearty version of a classic deli-style soup with both pungent dried mushrooms and fresh button mushrooms. Feel free to select your favorite dried mushroom to create your personal stamp; follow the same soaking directions. Even though this is a clear soup, the barley makes it a substantial dish.

❶ In a large soup pot, heat the olive oil over medium heat. Add the onions and leek and sauté for 3 to 5 minutes, or until softened. Add the celery, carrots, and shiitake and white mushrooms, and sauté for 3 to 5 minutes longer, or until slightly softened. Add the garlic and sauté for another minute. Add the barley and stock and bring to a boil. Cover, reduce the heat to medium-low, and simmer for about 1½ hours, or until the barley is tender but not mushy. ❷ Meanwhile, in a bowl, soak the dried mushrooms in the boiling water for 30 minutes. Drain, reserving the soaking liquid. Squeeze the mushrooms dry and cut them into ¼-inch cubes. Set aside. Strain the reserved liquid through a fine-mesh strainer to remove any grit. ❸ When the barley is cooked, add ½ cup of the strained liquid to the soup (reserve the remainder for another use or discard) along with the dried mushrooms and parsley and simmer for 5 more minutes. Taste for seasoning. ❹ To serve, ladle into soup bowls. Serve immediately.

Advance Preparation: Can be prepared up to 3 days ahead through step 2, covered, and refrigerated. Reheat gently. This soup also freezes well for up to 1 month. Adjust the seasonings when you reheat the frozen soup.

[SERVES 6 ➡ 8]

2 tablespoons olive oil

2 onions, finely chopped

1 leek, white and light green parts only,
    cleaned and coarsely chopped

2 stalks celery, coarsely chopped

3 carrots, peeled and coarsely chopped

¼ pound fresh shiitake mushrooms,
    sliced

½ pound fresh white button mushrooms,
    sliced

2 garlic cloves, minced

½ cup pearl barley

8 cups chicken stock

1 ounce dried porcini or morel mushrooms

2 cups boiling water

2 tablespoons finely chopped parsley

grilled seafood soup with ancho chile rouille

This adaptation of a Provençal-style fish stew is given a contemporary twist by grilling the seafood and adding an ancho chile to the rich *rouille*. Traditionally served with bouillabaisse, *rouille* (which means "rust") usually gets its heat from crushed red chile peppers. Ancho chile and a pinch of cayenne are used here instead, but you could also use a commercial sun-dried tomato paste or a Peeled Red Bell Pepper (page 177) if you can't find ancho chiles. Serve the colorful bisque with Mixed Greens with Roasted Beets and Toasted Walnuts (page 51) or any simple green salad, along with Herbed Garlic Cheese Bread (page 27) or a crusty French bread.

Ancho Chile Rouille

1 large ancho chile

2 cups boiling water

1 tablespoon olive oil

1 tablespoon fresh lime juice

½ teaspoon honey

½ cup mayonnaise

1 tablespoon Roasted Garlic Purée (page 175)

pinch of cayenne pepper

salt and white pepper

Bisque

2 tablespoons olive oil

2 leeks, white and light green parts only,
    cleaned and thinly sliced

1 carrot, peeled and finely chopped

3 garlic cloves

2 cups fish stock

2 cups dry white wine

1 can (28 ounces) diced tomatoes,
    with juice

pinch of saffron threads

salt and freshly ground black pepper

12 medium shrimp, peeled, with final tail
    segment intact, and deveined

12 medium sea scallops

2 tablespoons finely chopped chives,
    for garnish

❶ Prepare the *rouille*: In a small skillet, toast the chile over medium heat for 2 to 3 minutes, or until it begins to expand and the flesh is soft. (Turn on the overhead fan, since the chile may make you cough.) Remove from the heat and let cool. ❷ Wearing rubber gloves, slit open the chile and remove the seeds, the stem, and any veins. Place the chile in a small bowl and pour the boiling water over it to cover. Let stand for 15 minutes to soften. Remove the chile, reserving 2 tablespoons of the soaking water, and pat dry. ❸ In a food processor fitted with the metal blade, combine the chile, olive oil, lime juice, honey and the 2 tablespoons chile soaking water. Process until puréed, stopping to scrape down the sides of the work bowl several times. Strain the mixture through a fine-mesh strainer placed over a small bowl, pushing down on the chile mixture with a rubber spatula to extract all of the liquid from the coarse pieces. ❹ Add the mayonnaise, garlic purée, cayenne, salt, and white pepper to the chile mixture. Stir well to combine. Taste for seasoning. Cover and refrigerate until ready to use. ❺ Prepare the soup: Heat the olive oil in a large saucepan or Dutch oven over medium heat. Add the leeks and carrot and sauté for 3 to 5 minutes, or until softened. Add the garlic and sauté for another minute. Add the fish stock, wine, tomatoes, saffron, salt, and pepper and bring to a simmer. Cover partially and simmer over medium-low heat for 20 minutes. Taste for seasoning. ❻ Purée the soup in the pan with a hand blender or in batches in a food processor fitted with the metal blade, making sure to leave some texture. Return the soup to the pan if necessary. ❼ Heat an oiled grill pan over medium-high heat, or prepare a charcoal or gas grill for medium-high-heat grilling about 3 inches from the fire. Thread the shrimp and scallops onto 6 metal or bamboo skewers (soak bamboo in cold water for 30 minutes before grilling), and sprinkle lightly with salt and black pepper. Place the skewers on the grill, and grill for 3 to 4 minutes on each side, or until just cooked. Slide the seafood off skewers with the aid of a fork, place on a plate, and reserve. ❽ Reheat the soup over medium heat. Arrange 2 shrimp and 2 scallops in each shallow soup bowl. Ladle some warm bisque over the top. Top with a dollop of the *rouille* and garnish with the chives. Serve immediately.

Advance Preparation: Can be prepared up to 1 day ahead through step 6, covered, and refrigerated. Reheat gently and adjust the seasonings.

[SERVES 4 ➡ 6]

two-onion soup with parmesan-gruyère croutons

The key to good onion soup is the slow caramelizing of the onions so they will deliver an especially rich flavor. In this recipe, the onions are first roasted and then oven-braised in a rich broth. Beef stock is traditionally used for making onion soups, but chicken stock produces a lighter result that is still satisfying. If you like, vary the crouton topping by using different melting cheeses such as fresh goat cheese, teleme, or Italian Fontina. These little cheese croutons are easy to make and are not as heavy as the usual fondue-style onion soups.

2 tablespoons olive oil

4 large red onions, thinly sliced

4 leeks, white and light green parts only,
    cleaned and thinly sliced

salt and freshly ground black pepper

1 teaspoon sugar

10 cups chicken stock or beef stock

4 garlic cloves, minced

1 bay leaf

½ cup dry white wine

½ teaspoon minced fresh thyme or
    ¼ teaspoon dried

Parmesan-Gruyère Croutons

12 baguette slices, each ¼ inch thick

½ cup shredded Gruyère cheese

¼ cup freshly grated Parmesan cheese

2 tablespoons finely chopped parsley,
    for garnish

❶ Preheat the oven to 425 degrees F. In a large nonaluminum roasting pan, combine the olive oil, onions, leeks, salt, and pepper, and mix with a large spoon to coat all the ingredients evenly with the oil. Place in the oven and roast for 15 minutes, or until wilted. Using long oven mitts to protect your hands, stir in the sugar with the spoon. Continue roasting, stirring frequently, for 30 to 45 minutes longer, or until caramelized. (Use potholders when turning the onions.) ❷ Add the stock, garlic, bay leaf, white wine, and thyme to the onion mixture, again stirring well. Roast for an additional 30 minutes, or until the flavors are blended. Taste for seasoning. Remove the roasting pan from the oven and discard the bay leaf. Keep hot. ❸ Prepare the croutons: Preheat the broiler. Place the bread slices on a baking sheet and broil for 1½ to 2 minutes, or until golden. Watch carefully, as they burn easily. Meanwhile, in a small bowl, stir together the Gruyère and Parmesan cheeses. Sprinkle each bread slice with an equal amount of the cheese mixture, covering completely and reserving some of the cheese mixture for serving. Broil for 1 to 2 minutes, or until the cheeses are melted. ❹ To serve, ladle the soup into bowls and float 2 croutons on the top of each bowl. Sprinkle the remaining cheese mixture and a little chopped parsley over each soup bowl for garnish.

Advance Preparation: Can be prepared up to 3 days ahead through step 2, covered, and refrigerated. Reheat gently. This soup also freezes well for up to 1 month. Adjust the seasonings when you reheat the frozen soup.

[SERVES 6]

corn and tomato gazpacho

What began as a cold summertime soup in the Andalusia region of southern Spain has undergone countless variations on its journey through America. Traditional gazpacho revolves around a purée of vegetables, including tomatoes, bell peppers, onion, cucumber, and garlic. In this adaptation, the vegetables remain slightly crunchy and nontraditional ingredients such as anchovy paste, fresh sweet corn kernels, and sour cream liven the flavor and texture of the chilled soup. Restaurants across the country have taken liberties with this simple Iberian soup, even transforming it into a sauce to serve over fish. I like to serve it as a prelude to Country Chicken Salad Niçoise (page 45).

❶ In a large bowl, stir the anchovy paste into the V-8 juice until dissolved. Add the tomatoes, chicken stock, olive oil, vinegar, garlic, salt, and pepper, and whisk until blended. Add the cucumbers, onion, and basil and mix well. Add all but 1 tablespoon each of the chopped red and yellow bell peppers (reserve for garnish). ❷ Purée 3 cups of the mixture in a blender and return it to the bowl. Add the corn, stirring well to blend. Cover and refrigerate for at least 4 hours, or until well chilled. ❸ Just before serving, in a small bowl, whisk together the ¼ cup sour cream with 1 cup of the tomato mixture until blended. Add to the large bowl of soup and whisk vigorously. Taste for seasoning. ❹ To serve, ladle into soup bowls and garnish with the reserved chopped peppers, the sour cream, and the chopped basil.

Advance Preparation: Can be prepared up to 1 day ahead through step 2, covered, and refrigerated. Adjust the seasonings.

[SERVES 6 ➡ 8]

2 teaspoons anchovy paste

4 cups V-8 juice

2½ pounds ripe tomatoes, peeled, seeded, and finely chopped

2 cups chicken stock

2 tablespoons olive oil

2 tablespoons red wine vinegar

3 garlic cloves, minced

salt and freshly ground black pepper

2 cucumbers, peeled, halved lengthwise, seeded, and finely chopped

3 tablespoons finely chopped red onion

¼ cup finely chopped fresh basil

1 small red bell pepper, seeded and finely chopped

1 small yellow bell pepper, seeded and finely chopped

1 cup corn kernels (about 2 ears of corn)

¼ cup sour cream

Garnish

½ cup sour cream

2 tablespoons finely chopped fresh basil

chilled herbed cucumber soup

This easy chilled soup combines the smoothness of yogurt and buttermilk with the crunch of shredded cucumber and toasted almonds. The result is a wonderful balance of texture and flavor, heightened by plenty of fresh herbs. European cucumbers, cultivated in hothouses and usually sold tightly wrapped in plastic, are much longer than field-grown cucumbers and are available year-round. This hothouse variety is virtually seedless and does not require peeling.

3 tablespoons slivered blanched almonds

1½ cups nonfat plain yogurt

1½ cups buttermilk

¼ cup sour cream

1 European cucumber, shredded

¼ cup finely chopped parsley

2 garlic cloves, minced

3 tablespoons finely chopped fresh mint

3 tablespoons finely chopped fresh dill

salt and white pepper

❶ Heat a small skillet over low heat. Add the almonds and toast, tossing often, for 2 to 3 minutes, or until golden. Remove to a plate and reserve. ❷ In a bowl, stir together the yogurt, buttermilk, and sour cream until well blended. Add the cucumber, parsley, garlic, mint, dill, salt, and white pepper. Cover and refrigerate for about 2 hours, or until chilled. ❸ Taste for seasoning. Pour into chilled soup bowls and garnish with the toasted almonds.

Advance Preparation: Can be prepared up to 8 hours ahead through step 2, covered, and refrigerated. Adjust the seasonings.

[SERVES 6]

country chicken salade niçoise

This poached-chicken salad is a variation on France's classic *salade niçoise*, which uses tuna. It is an excellent way to showcase fresh vegetables, since the dressing is simple enough to allow the flavors of the crisp vegetables to come through. Serve this salad on a big white platter surrounded with spears of romaine and with Parmesan Crisps (page 26) spread with a spoonful of Two-Olive Spread (page 22). Begin with Chilled Herbed Cucumber Soup (page 44) if the weather is warm, White Bean Soup with Tomatoes and Spinach (page 32) on a chilly day.

❶ Prepare the salad: In a large saucepan, bring the chicken stock to a simmer over medium-high heat. There should be enough liquid to cover the chicken. Add the chicken and simmer for 12 to 15 minutes, or until just tender. Remove from the heat and let the chicken cool in the liquid. Drain and remove the skin. Shred the chicken into bite-sized pieces and place in a large mixing bowl. ❷ Bring a large pot of water to a boil. Add the potatoes and cook for 20 to 30 minutes, or until tender but slightly resistant when pierced with a knife. Drain and let cool. When cool, cut into quarters and add to the chicken. ❸ Meanwhile, bring another saucepan of water to a boil. Add the asparagus and cook for 2 minutes, or until just tender but still crisp. Drain and place the asparagus in ice water to cover. When cool, drain and add to the chicken and potatoes along with the tomatoes, olives, capers, and basil. ❹ Prepare the dressing: In a small bowl, combine the garlic, mustard, lemon juice, and parsley. Slowly whisk in the olive oil until thoroughly incorporated. Add salt and pepper and taste for seasoning. ❺ To serve, add enough of the dressing to the chicken mixture to moisten it evenly. Toss carefully to combine. Serve on a platter as directed in the recipe introduction, or arrange the romaine spears in shallow individual bowls, spoon the salad into the bowls and drizzle with more dressing, if desired. Serve at once.

Advance Preparation: Can be prepared up to 8 hours ahead through step 4, covered, and refrigerated.

[SERVES 4 ➡ 6]

Salad

3 cups chicken stock

2 whole chicken breasts, halved and boned

1 pound red new potatoes

½ pound pencil-thin asparagus, trimmed
  and cut on the diagonal into
  1½-inch lengths

Ice water, as needed

12 cherry tomatoes, halved

12 yellow teardrop tomatoes

½ cup Niçoise olives, rinsed and drained

2 tablespoons capers, rinsed and drained

2 tablespoons finely chopped fresh basil

Dressing

2 garlic cloves, minced

2 teaspoons Dijon mustard

¼ cup fresh lemon juice

1 tablespoon finely chopped parsley

½ cup olive oil

salt and freshly ground black pepper

1 head romaine lettuce, outer dark green
  leaves removed

grilled tomatillo chicken salad
with creamy pumpkin seed dressing

A low-fat, creamy dressing makes this Mexican-influenced salad a perfect main course for a summer evening. Tomatillo salsa is used as a marinade to tenderize the chicken and give it a slightly piquant flavor when grilled. I like to begin with Chilled Herbed Cucumber Soup (page 44). For dessert try Peach and Plum Crostata (page 141).

❶ Prepare the dressing: In a blender, combine all the ingredients and blend until smooth. Taste for seasoning. Transfer to a glass jar and refrigerate. ❷ Prepare the salad: If using a grill pan, flatten the breasts by placing them between 2 sheets of plastic wrap and pounding them with a meat pounder or the flat side of a cleaver. Place the chicken breasts in a shallow nonaluminum pan, pour the Tomatillo Salsa over them, and turn them to coat evenly. Cover and refrigerate for 2 to 4 hours. ❸ Prepare a charcoal or gas grill for medium-high-heat grilling about 3 inches from the fire, or place a lightly oiled grill pan over medium-high heat. Remove the chicken from the marinade and grill for 7 to 10 minutes on each side on the charcoal or gas grill or 5 minutes on each side on the grill pan, or until cooked through. Transfer the chicken to a cutting board and cut on the diagonal into ½-inch-thick slices. ❹ To serve, arrange the salad greens in a large bowl. Top with the chicken strips, then scatter the corn, jicama, tomatoes, and pepitas over the top. Pour enough dressing over the salad to moisten, and toss. Serve the remaining dressing on the side.

Advance Preparation: Can be prepared up to 4 hours ahead through step 2. Dressing can be prepared up to 2 days ahead, covered, and refrigerated.

[SERVES 6]

Creamy Pumpkin Seed Dressing

2 tablespoons salted roasted pepitas

1 cup buttermilk

1 tablespoon fresh lemon juice

1 tablespoon fresh lime juice

3 tablespoons freshly grated Parmesan cheese

1 garlic clove, minced

1 ½ tablespoons finely chopped cilantro

1 teaspoon grainy mustard

5 tablespoons olive oil

salt and freshly ground black pepper

Salad

2 whole chicken breasts, skinned, boned and halved

1 recipe Tomatillo Salsa (page 183)

2 heads romaine lettuce, outer dark green leaves removed, torn into bite-sized pieces

½ cup fresh corn kernels (about 1 ear of corn)

½ cup diced jicama

6 cherry tomatoes, halved

2 tablespoons salted roasted pepitas

asian noodle salad with shrimp and snow peas

America's fascination with pasta salads has taken the nation's cooks a long way from the old-fashioned macaroni salad that traditionally graced tables from Hawaii to New York. Stop by an Asian grocery store to choose from shelves of Chinese wheat noodles, made with or without eggs, or simply use dried linguine. Either way, the cool mint leaves and lime juice offset the noodles and add a light, citrus-enhanced flavor to the shrimp and vegetables.

You can blanch the carrots by immersing them in boiling water for 1 minute and refreshing them under cold water if you prefer a more refined flavor. Serve this salad as a main course, beginning with Purée of Vegetable Soup with Pesto Swirl (page 38) and ending with Lemon Meringue Tart with Macadamia Crust (page 146).

1 pound dried Chinese wheat noodles
    or linguine
1 tablespoon vegetable oil

Dressing

¼ cup vegetable oil
2 teaspoons dark sesame oil
¼ cup rice wine vinegar
1 tablespoon fresh lime juice
1 tablespoon honey
2 garlic cloves, minced
1½ teaspoons minced fresh ginger
1 tablespoon finely chopped fresh basil
3 tablespoons finely chopped fresh mint
salt

1 pound medium shrimp, peeled
    and deveined
3 carrots, peeled and cut into matchsticks
2 ounces snow peas, trimmed and sliced
    lengthwise into 2-inch strips
1 small head romaine lettuce, thinly sliced

Garnish

3 scallions, white and lighter green parts
    only, thinly sliced
lime wedges
fresh mint sprigs

❶ Bring a large pot of water to a boil over medium-high heat. Add the noodles and boil for about 7 minutes, or until barely tender and still firm. Drain the noodles immediately and rinse them with cold water until cooled. Drain again, place in a large bowl, and toss well with the vegetable oil so they don't stick together. ❷ Prepare the dressing: In a small bowl, combine all the ingredients and whisk to blend well. Cover and refrigerate. ❸ Bring another large pot of water to a boil over high heat. Add the shrimp and cook until they just change color, about 1 minute. Drain and rinse immediately with cold water until cooled. Drain well. ❹ Pour the dressing over the noodles and toss to coat. Add the shrimp, carrots, and snow peas, and toss again. Taste for seasoning. ❺ To serve, arrange the romaine lettuce on a serving platter or in individual shallow bowls. Place the noodles over the lettuce. Garnish with the scallions, lime wedges, and mint sprigs.

Advance Preparation: Can be prepared up to 4 hours ahead through step 4, covered, and refrigerated. The dressing can be prepared up to 1 day ahead, covered, and refrigerated.

[SERVES 6 ➡ 8]

Pictured on page 31

wilted greens with grilled portobello mushrooms and dried cherry vinaigrette

The French technique of cultivating mushrooms was adopted by growers in New York during the late-nineteenth century. Today, the American mushroom industry is thriving, and mushroom producers are cultivating "wild mushrooms" as well as the common white button variety. The portobello mushroom is actually the fully mature aremina, a variety of white button mushroom

Since portobellos tend to dry out when grilled, it is important to marinate them for at least an hour before cooking. The earthy, meaty flavor of these fungi stands up well to the dressing of strong vinegar and tart dried cherries. A variety of lettuces, baby spinach, and frisée works well here.

❶ In a small bowl, whisk together the balsamic vinegar, garlic, olive oil, salt, and pepper. Arrange the mushroom caps in a single layer in a shallow nonaluminum dish and pour the vinegar marinade over the mushrooms. Cover and let stand for 1 hour, turning the caps after 30 minutes. ❷ Place the salad greens in a large salad bowl and set aside. ❸ Lightly oil a grill pan over medium-high heat. Remove the mushrooms from the marinade, place on the hot grill, and use a skillet or other weight to press down on the mushrooms. Sear the mushrooms for 2 minutes on each side, or until tender. Transfer the mushrooms to a cutting board, slice thinly, and add to the lettuce. ❹ Prepare the vinaigrette: Heat the olive oil in a skillet over medium heat. Add the shallots and sauté for about 2 minutes, or until softened. Add the vinegar and boil for 1 minute. Add the dried cherries, salt, and pepper, and heat through for 1 minute longer. Taste for seasoning. ❺ To serve, pour the hot vinaigrette over the lettuce and mushrooms and toss to coat all the ingredients evenly. ❻ Arrange the salad on individual plates and sprinkle the goat cheese evenly over the tops. Serve immediately.

Advance Preparation: Can be prepared up to 4 hours ahead through step 3, covered, and refrigerated. Remove from the refrigerator 30 minutes before continuing.

[SERVES 4 ➡ 6]

½ pound mixed salad greens
2 tablespoons balsamic vinegar
4 garlic cloves, minced
¼ cup olive oil
salt and freshly ground black pepper
½ pound fresh portobello mushrooms,
    stems trimmed
olive oil, for grilling

Dried Cherry Vinaigrette
½ cup olive oil
2 shallots, finely chopped
⅓ cup sherry vinegar or red wine vinegar
¼ cup pitted dried cherries
Salt and freshly ground black pepper

¼ cup fresh goat cheese, crumbled

american bistro caesar salad
with roasted garlic dressing

Caesar salad epitomizes American bistro cooking since it calls for only a few highly flavorful ingredients to be tossed together, often tableside, and served immediately. It worked for Caesar Cardini when he needed a quick dish for hungry patrons in his Tijuana restaurant back in 1924, and it still works today, even with a few alterations.

This modern version of the classic Caesar is packed with color and flavor. Roasted Garlic Purée is used in the dressing in place of the usual raw egg, and instead of the expected romaine leaves, butter lettuce and purplish red radicchio are combined in the bowl. Serve alongside grilled fish and soups, or alone as a light lunch.

Roasted Garlic Dressing

1 tablespoon Roasted Garlic Purée
    (page 175)
¼ cup fresh lemon juice
1 to 2 teaspoons anchovy paste, to taste
¼ teaspoon freshly ground black pepper
½ cup olive oil
¼ cup freshly grated Parmesan cheese

1 head radicchio, torn into bite-sized pieces
1 head butter lettuce, torn into bite-
    sized pieces
12 Parmesan Crisps (page 26)
Wedge of Parmesan cheese, for garnish

❶ Prepare the dressing: In a food processor fitted with the metal blade, combine the garlic purée, lemon juice, anchovy paste, and pepper, and process to combine. With the motor running, add the olive oil in a slow, steady stream and process until emulsified. Whisk in the Parmesan cheese. Taste for seasoning. ❷ To serve: In a large bowl, combine the radicchio and butter lettuce. Drizzle the dressing over the top and toss well. Add the Parmesan Crisps, breaking them into smaller pieces, and toss again. Arrange the salad on individual plates. Holding the wedge of Parmesan over each plate, use a vegetable peeler to shave off large curls of cheese, letting them fall into the salads.

Advance Preparation:
The Parmesan Crisps can be prepared up to 3 days ahead and stored in an airtight container at room temperature. The dressing can be prepared up to 1 day ahead, covered, and refrigerated.

[SERVES 4 ➡ 6]

mixed greens with roasted beets and toasted walnuts

Here, roasted beets are cooled, sliced, and arranged atop mixed greens for a colorful salad. Crisp pancetta, toasted walnuts, and crumbled feta add bursts of flavor and texture to the dressed greens. This makes a splendid beginning to Roasted Rack of Lamb with Herbed Crust (page 102), Braised Spinach (page 125), and Roasted New Potatoes with Leeks (page 133).

❶ Prepare the dressing: In a small bowl, combine the shallot, mustard, lemon juice, and balsamic vinegar, and whisk to blend. Slowly add the olive oil, whisking until blended. Add the salt and pepper and taste for seasoning. Reserve. ❷ Prepare the salad: Heat a skillet over medium heat. Add the walnuts and toast, tossing often, for 2 to 3 minutes, or until they begin to brown slightly. Remove from the heat and set aside. ❸ In the same skillet, sauté the pancetta over medium heat, turning to cook evenly, for about 5 minutes, or until browned and crisp. Using a slotted utensil, transfer the pancetta to paper towels to drain. ❹ Place the salad greens in a large bowl. Drizzle half of the dressing over the greens and toss to coat evenly. Arrange the salad greens on individual plates. Decorate with the beets and finish with the toasted walnuts, pancetta, and feta. Serve the remaining dressing on the side.

Advance Preparation: Can be prepared up to 4 hours ahead through step 2 and kept at room temperature. The beets can be prepared 2 days ahead, covered, and refrigerated.

[SERVES 4 ➡ 6]

Dressing
1 shallot, finely chopped
1 tablespoon grainy mustard
2 tablespoons fresh lemon juice
2 tablespoons balsamic vinegar
½ cup olive oil
salt and freshly ground black pepper

Salad
⅓ cup walnuts, coarsely chopped
4 slices pancetta, coarsely chopped
½ pound mixed salad greens
2 Basic Roasted Beets (page 178), cut into matchsticks
¼ cup crumbled feta cheese

chopped winter salad with lemon-mint dressing

This colorful salad features winter's best vegetables in an uncomplicated, yet highly flavorful cold-weather slaw. Lemon juice adds a clean flavor to the fennel and cabbage, and sweetened dried cranberries perfectly punctuate the tart dressing. Follow this with Ragout of Beef with Sun-Dried Tomatoes and Winter Vegetables (page 90) for a satisfying winter meal. This salad is also great on a buffet with Southwestern-Style Beef Chili (page 95).

Lemon-Mint Dressing

2 garlic cloves, minced

⅓ cup fresh lemon juice

1½ teaspoons sugar

salt and freshly ground black pepper

½ cup olive oil

2 tablespoons finely chopped fresh mint

Salad

½ green cabbage, finely shredded

2 fennel bulbs, trimmed and
    finely shredded

4 carrots, peeled and shredded

1 tablespoon chopped cilantro

1 tablespoon chopped fresh dill

¼ cup sweetened dried cranberries,
    for garnish

❶ Prepare the dressing: In a small bowl, whisk together the garlic, lemon juice, sugar, salt, and pepper. Slowly add the olive oil, whisking until blended. Stir in the mint. Taste for seasoning. ❷ Prepare the salad: In a large bowl, combine the cabbage, fennel, carrots, cilantro, and dill, and toss to combine. ❸ Drizzle the dressing over the salad and toss to coat evenly. Sprinkle the dried cranberries over the top.

Advance Preparation: Can be prepared up to 4 hours ahead, covered, and refrigerated.

[SERVES 6 ➡ 8]

green bean, sweet pepper, and jicama salad

There are certain salads that have become modern standards in American bistro cooking, and this combination of crisp, sweet vegetables, inspired by the French crudité-style salads, is one of them. Be creative with this recipe, using it as a jumping off point for showcasing your favorite vegetables. Other good ideas include mushrooms, zucchini, asparagus, or teardrop tomatoes.

I like to serve the salad as a light side dish to grilled chicken or Grilled Entrecôte (page 93). It is also excellent combined with cooled Herbed Vegetable Rice (page 113) for a satisfying and very colorful vegetable rice salad. Start with Tomato Bisque (page 34) and serve the rice salad with fresh Parmesan cheese shavings on top.

❶ Bring a saucepan full of water to a boil. Place the green beans in a kitchen strainer basket with a handle for easy lifting out, and lower into the boiling water. Cook for 7 to 10 minutes, depending on their size. The beans should be slightly crisp to the bite. Lift out the green beans and immerse in the ice water to stop the cooking. Drain well and place in a bowl. Repeat with the carrots, placing them in the strainer basket and cooking for about 2 minutes in the boiling water, or until crisp-tender. Lift out the carrots and immerse in the ice water to stop the cooking. Drain well and place in the bowl with the green beans. ❷ Add the bell pepper, jicama, and tomatoes to the vegetables. ❸ Prepare the dressing: In a small bowl, whisk together the mustard, lemon juice, and chives. Slowly add the olive oil, whisking until blended. Add salt and pepper and taste for seasoning. ❹ Drizzle the dressing over the vegetables and toss to combine. Taste for seasoning. Cover and refrigerate for at least 1 hour before serving.

Advance Preparation: Can be prepared up to 1 day ahead, covered, and refrigerated. Adjust the seasonings.

[SERVES 6]

1 pound green beans, trimmed

ice water, as needed

2 carrots, peeled and cut into matchsticks

1 yellow or red bell pepper, seeded and cut
      into matchsticks

½ pound jicama, peeled and cut into
      matchsticks

10 cherry tomatoes, halved

Dressing

1 teaspoon Dijon mustard

¼ cup fresh lemon juice

1 teaspoon finely chopped fresh chives

½ cup olive oil

salt and freshly ground black pepper

orzo salad with tomatoes, basil, and feta

Orzo is a tiny, almond-shaped pasta that resembles rice. It is particularly well-suited for cold salads because of its texture and size. This easy pasta salad is a perfect companion for fish, or an ideal main course on its own. The toasted pine nuts and tomatoes balance the saltiness of the feta cheese and olives, and the lemon dressing brings all the elements together. This is best eaten the same day it is prepared.

½ cup pine nuts

3 cups orzo

3 tomatoes, peeled, seeded, and diced

¾ cup Kalamata olives, pitted
    and halved

¼ cup finely chopped parsley

¼ cup fresh lemon juice

½ cup olive oil

salt and freshly ground black pepper

1¼ cups crumbled feta cheese

½ cup finely chopped fresh basil

❶ Heat a small skillet over medium-low heat. Add the pine nuts and toast, tossing often, for 2 to 3 minutes, or until lightly browned. Remove to a plate and reserve. ❷ Bring a large pot full of water to a boil. Add the orzo and cook for 6 to 8 minutes, or until al dente. Drain, cool under cold running water, and drain well again. Pour the cooled orzo into a bowl. ❸ Add the tomatoes, olives, and parsley to the orzo and mix together. ❹ In a small bowl, whisk together the lemon juice and olive oil. Add the salt and pepper and taste for seasoning. Pour the dressing over the orzo and stir gently to incorporate. Cover and refrigerate for at least 30 minutes. ❺ When ready to serve, add the feta, the toasted pine nuts, and basil to the orzo, mix together, and adjust the seasoning.

Advance Preparation: Can be prepared up to 4 hours ahead, covered, and refrigerated. Adjust the seasonings.

[SERVES 6 ➡ 8]

corn salad with cherry tomatoes

There is nothing like corn in the summer, especially when it is so garden-fresh, sweet, and tender that it doesn't even need cooking. Look for fresh, green husks and tender, milky kernels that are plump and leave no space between the rows. Hold the corn cob upright, at a slight angle to the cutting board, and use a sharp paring knife to cut off the kernels.

Vine-ripened cherry tomatoes, fragrant herbs, and a dash of olive oil accentuate the sweet corn and together make a colorful summer salad to serve alongside barbecued meats and poultry. This recipe is simple, yet it epitomizes the clean flavors characteristic of bistro cooking. If you can't eat corn the same day it is picked, store the ears in the refrigerator for a short time. Waiting too long will cause the delicious natural sugars to turn to starch.

❶ In a bowl, combine the corn, tomatoes, basil, and chives, and stir to mix. Drizzle with the olive oil and add the salt and pepper. Stir to combine and taste for seasoning. ❷ Serve the salad at room temperature, or refrigerate and serve chilled.

Advance Preparation: Can be prepared up to 4 hours ahead, covered, and refrigerated.

[SERVES 4 ➡ 6]

3 cups white or yellow corn kernels
    (about 6 ears of corn)
20 cherry tomatoes, quartered
2 tablespoons finely chopped fresh basil
1 tablespoon finely chopped chives
1 tablespoon olive oil
salt and freshly ground black pepper

quinoa and cracked wheat vegetable salad

Grain salads seem to have come full circle in modern American cooking. In the 1960s, the health-food movement introduced salads with lentils, wheatberries, and bulgur. Tabbouleh made with bulgur, olive oil, lemon, mint, tomato, and parsley became a mainstay first in health-food stores and later in delis across the country. But these salads fell out of fashion during the nouvelle cuisine and California cuisine movements. Happily, the fascination with grain salads has returned, with many new combinations. This version blends quinoa with cracked wheat, vegetables, and feta. The result is a flavorful and highly nutritious salad that can be made ahead and refrigerated until ready to serve.

Quinoa comes from the Andes and is referred to as a "super grain" since it is nearly a complete protein and is very high in calcium. The seeds are covered with a natural bitter substance called saponin, so they must be rinsed well prior to cooking. This salad is excellent served with Grilled Citrus Chicken with *Raita* Sauce (page 77) for a dinner, or with Roasted Butternut Squash–Sweet Potato Soup with Herbed Sour Cream (page 37) for a hearty lunch.

Salad

10 cuts water

1 cup medium cracked wheat

1 cup quinoa

2 tablespoons finely chopped red onion

¼ pound green beans, trimmed and
    finely chopped

1 carrot, peeled and finely diced

3 tablespoons finely chopped parsley

1 tablespoon finely chopped chives

Dressing

¾ cup Herb Vinaigrette (page 176)

3 tablespoons fresh lemon juice

salt and freshly ground black pepper

¾ cup crumbled feta cheese

❶ Prepare the salad: Bring 2 cups of the water to a boil. Place the cracked wheat in a heatproof bowl and pour the boiling water over it. Let stand until the wheat absorbs the water. This should take about 1 hour. ❷ Meanwhile, pour the quinoa into a bowl of cold water and rinse well, rubbing it between your hands. Drain and repeat until the water is clear. In a large saucepan, bring the remaining water to a boil over high heat. Add the quinoa, stir once and return to a boil. Reduce the heat to medium and cook, uncovered, for 10 minutes or until tender. Drain well with a fine-mesh strainer. Transfer to a large bowl. ❸ Drain the cracked wheat in a colander. Transfer to a dry tea towel and wring out any excess liquid. Place in the bowl with the quinoa. ❹ Add the onion, green beans, and carrots to the grains. Mix with a fork to keep the quinoa and wheat fluffy. Add the parsley and chives. ❺ Prepare the dressing: In a small bowl, whisk together all the ingredients, blending well. Taste for seasoning. ❻ Pour the dressing over the grains and vegetables and mix with the fork. Sprinkle the feta cheese over the top and gently toss and stir to incorporate evenly. Taste for seasoning and serve.

Advance Preparation: Can be prepared up to 8 hours ahead, covered, and refrigerated.

[SERVES 6 ➡ 8]

Seafood

whole roasted striped bass on sliced potatoes

Roasting a whole fish may sound like a daunting task, but the process is surprisingly easy. First, locate a good source for fresh fish (Asian markets are generally ideal), and select fish that show signs of freshness: clear eyes; moist-looking, firm flesh; and free of strong odors (fish should smell like the ocean). High-heat roasting assures a crisp skin and moist interior. White Rose potatoes (or any medium-sized white-fleshed potatoes with thin tan skin) work best in this dish because they keep their texture and cook evenly. Serve the fish atop its bed of sliced and roasted potatoes on a large serving platter for a dramatic presentation. This is wonderful with Braised Spinach (page 125).

2 striped bass, 1½ pounds each, cleaned
    with head and tail intact

¼ cup olive oil

2 tablespoons fresh lemon juice

1 garlic clove, minced

1 teaspoon salt, plus salt to taste

freshly ground black pepper

8 to 10 large fresh basil leaves

2½ pounds White Rose potatoes
    (see recipe introduction)

1 lemon, sliced

Garnish

juice of 1 lemon

2 tablespoons basil oil, plus extra
    for serving

3 scallions, white and light green parts
    only, thinly sliced

[SERVES 4]

❶ Rinse the fish thoroughly inside and out under cold running water to clean off any blood. Cut three diagonal slashes on each side of each fish. Set the fish in a shallow baking dish, letting the heads and tails hang over the sides a little if necessary. ❷ Rub 2 tablespoons of the olive oil, the lemon juice, garlic and the 1 teaspoon salt into the sides and cavities of the fish. Sprinkle the cavities with pepper and stuff with the basil leaves, dividing them equally. Cover and refrigerate for 20 to 30 minutes. ❸ Preheat the oven to 500 degrees F. Lightly coat a large roasting pan with nonstick cooking spray. Cut the potatoes into slices ¼ inch thick and place in the roasting pan. Drizzle with the remaining 2 tablespoons olive oil and toss to coat well. Sprinkle with salt and pepper, toss again, and spread out in an even layer in the pan. Roast the potatoes, stirring every 5 minutes, for 15 to 20 minutes, or until they begin to get brown and crispy. ❹ Remove the pan from the oven. Gently lift the fish from the baking dish and place them at an angle, side by side, on top of the roasted potatoes. Arrange the lemon slices on top of the fish. Roast for 10 minutes per inch of thickness at the thickest part of the fish, about 15 minutes for a 1½-pound fish. ❺ Carefully move the fish aside and transfer the potatoes to a serving platter large enough to accommodate the fish. Use a metal spatula to scrape the crisp, brown pieces off the bottom of the pan onto the platter. ❻ Transfer the fish to a large plate and fillet: Starting at the neck, slit the skin along the back down to the tail. Then cut down to the bone behind the head. Open up the fish and gently lift the bone off the flesh, removing any remaining belly bones. Repeat with the second fish. Fold the top fillet back over so that the fish is whole once again. Place the fish on top of the potatoes, drizzle with the lemon juice and the 2 tablespoons basil oil, and sprinkle with the scallions. To serve, cut the fish into individual pieces and pass extra basil oil.

broiled snapper with poblano chile pesto

A pestolike poblano chile glaze elevates the simple flavor of snapper to a spicy, festive meal. If you can't get snapper, substitute fresh orange roughy, sole, or lingcod. For an added twist, serve the snapper alongside Grilled Polenta (page 112) and stir a tablespoon of the pesto into the hot polenta prior to grilling.

The dark green poblano ranges from mild to medium hot, making it a perfect spicy counterpoint to the sweet corn in the polenta. The versatile pesto can also be used as a flavoring for mashed potatoes, or brushed onto chicken for grilling. Other good side-dish matches include Spicy Black Beans with Island Salsa (page 118) or Herbed Vegetable Rice (page 113).

❶ Prepare the pesto: With the motor running, add the pepitas, peeled chile, and garlic cloves to a blender or a food processor fitted with the metal blade. Process until puréed. With the motor still running, add the cilantro, parsley, and lime juice, and process until puréed. With the motor running, slowly pour in the olive oil in a fine stream and process until well blended. Add salt and pepper to taste. If making polenta (see recipe introduction), remove 1 tablespoon of the pesto to swirl into the polenta. Spoon the remaining pesto into a small bowl, add the mayonnaise, and stir well to combine. You should have about ½ cup. ❷ Preheat the broiler. Lightly coat a shallow broiler pan with nonstick cooking spray. Arrange the snapper fillets on the pan and season with salt and pepper. Broil the fish about 3 inches from the heat for 3 minutes. Using a large spatula, carefully turn the fish, then spread the pesto evenly over it. Return to the broiler and broil for about 3 more minutes or until bubbly, well browned, and just cooked through. Be careful the fish does not burn. ❸ Using the spatula, remove the fish from the broiler pan, taking care not to break the pieces. Arrange the fish atop the polenta, if using. Garnish with cilantro leaves and serve immediately.

Advance Preparation: The pesto can be prepared up to 1 day ahead, covered, and refrigerated. Bring to room temperature before spreading on the fish.

[SERVES 4]

Poblano Chile Pesto

3 tablespoons salted, roasted pepitas
½ Peeled Poblano Chile (page 177), coarsely chopped
2 garlic cloves
¼ cup firmly packed cilantro leaves
½ cup firmly packed Italian parsley leaves
1 tablespoon fresh lime juice
1 tablespoon olive oil
salt and freshly ground black pepper
2 tablespoons mayonnaise

4 fresh snapper fillets, 6 to 8 ounces each
salt and freshly ground black pepper

cilantro leaves, for garnish

grilled swordfish with island salsa

The mild flavor and firm, meatlike texture of swordfish make it ideal for grilling. The bright, tangy salsa creates a colorful topping perfect for this quick dish. Begin with Green Bean, Sweet Pepper, and Jicama Salad (page 53) and serve the swordfish with Herbed Vegetable Rice (page 113).

❶ Prepare the marinade: In a small bowl, stir together all the ingredients, mixing well. Taste for seasoning. ❷ Arrange the swordfish steaks in a shallow nonaluminum dish and pour the marinade over the top. Turn to coat both sides evenly. Cover and refrigerate for 30 minutes to 2 hours. ❸ Prepare a charcoal or gas grill for medium-high-heat grilling about 3 inches from the fire, or heat a lightly oiled grill pan over medium-high heat. Remove the swordfish from the marinade, place on the grill, and grill for 4 to 5 minutes on each side, or until just cooked through. ❹ To serve, top each swordfish steak with an equal amount of the salsa. Serve immediately.

Advance Preparation: Can be prepared up to 2 hours ahead through step 2.

[SERVES 6]

Marinade

3 tablespoons olive oil

2 teaspoons finely chopped lime zest

½ cup fresh lime juice

2 garlic cloves, minced

1 teaspoon minced fresh ginger

1 teaspoon soy sauce

salt and freshly ground black pepper

6 swordfish steaks, 6 to 8 ounces each

1 cup Island Salsa (page 184)

grilled halibut with eggplant-olive caponata

Caponata, the Sicilian appetizer, is usually served on toasted croutons. Here it becomes a bold, colorful sauce that complements the delicate halibut. Contrasting flavors are the key to this sauce. Select a rich black olive, such as a Kalamata, or a strong-flavored green olive to maximize the depth of flavor. Halibut is a white, mild-flavored flatfish caught in northern Pacific and Atlantic waters. For a casual American bistro presentation, serve this Mediterranean-inspired dish in shallow white soup bowls and garnish it with a sprinkling of fresh herbs.

Marinade

1 tablespoon finely chopped chives

1 garlic clove, minced

2 tablespoons dry white wine

2 tablespoons olive oil

4 skinned halibut fillets, 6 to 8 ounces each

Sauce

2 tablespoons olive oil

1 eggplant, unpeeled, sliced lengthwise into
⅓-inch-thick slices

1 leek, white and light green parts only,
cleaned and thinly sliced

2 garlic cloves, minced

2 large tomatoes, peeled, seeded, and finely
chopped

½ cup chicken stock

½ cup dry white wine

1 tablespoon balsamic vinegar

1 teaspoon dark brown sugar

pinch of crushed red pepper flakes

⅓ cup pitted black olives, such as
Kalamata, or green olives, rinsed,
drained, and thinly sliced

1 tablespoon capers, rinsed and drained

¼ cup golden raisins

salt and freshly ground black pepper

1 tablespoon finely chopped chives,
for garnish

❶ Prepare the marinade: In a small bowl, combine all the ingredients and whisk to blend well. ❷ Arrange the fish fillets in a shallow nonaluminum dish and pour the marinade over the top. Turn the fillets to coat both sides evenly. Cover and refrigerate for from 30 minutes to 2 hours. ❸ Prepare the sauce: Prepare a charcoal or gas grill for medium-high-heat grilling about 3 inches from the fire, or heat a lightly oiled grill pan over medium-high heat. Using 1 tablespoon of the olive oil, brush both sides of the eggplant slices. Place the eggplant slices on the grill and grill for 2 to 3 minutes on each side, or until grill marks appear and the eggplant is very tender. Transfer to a cutting board and cut into ¼-inch pieces. ❹ In a large skillet, heat the remaining 1 tablespoon olive oil over medium-high heat. Add the leek and sauté for 3 to 5 minutes, or until softened. Add the garlic and sauté for 1 minute longer. Add the tomatoes, stock, white wine, vinegar, brown sugar, and pepper flakes and bring to a simmer. Reduce the heat to low, cover, and cook for 10 minutes. Add the eggplant, olives, capers, raisins, salt, and pepper and cook for 3 minutes. Taste for seasoning. Keep warm. ❺ Remove the halibut from the marinade and season with salt and pepper. Using the same charcoal or gas grill or grill pan prepared for medium-high heat, grill the halibut about 3 inches from the fire 4 to 5 minutes on each side, or until just cooked through. ❻ To serve, spoon the warm sauce into individual shallow bowls, dividing it equally. Cut each halibut fillet in half. Place one-half of the fillet on the sauce, arranging it horizontally. Place the remaining fillet half at an angle on top of the first half. Garnish with the chives and serve immediately.

Advance Preparation: Can be prepared up to 2 hours ahead through step 2. The sauce can be prepared up to 1 day ahead, covered, and refrigerated. Bring to room temperature before continuing and reheat just before serving.

[SERVES 4]

spicy clam stew with roasted garlic, shallots, tomatoes, and white wine

Fresh clams are served here in a light tomato broth accented with garlic and white wine. Choose from sweet Manila clams that are grown in the Pacific Northwest, or tender, plump littleneck clams from the East Coast. When purchased, live clams should have tightly closed shells, or slightly open shells that spring shut quickly when tapped, indicating their freshness.

Clamped inside those shells is the salty, grayish ocean water that could spill into your steaming broth when the clams cook and open. One way to prevent this from happening is to "feed" the clams cornmeal as they briefly sit in fresh water, encouraging them to open their shells, take in clean water, and flush out the briny water. This quick process can make an enormous difference in the final flavor of the dish.

As a variation, spoon the clams and sauce over hot linguine. This recipe also works well with greenish-shelled New Zealand mussels.

❶ Clean the clams by scrubbing them with a brush under cold running water to remove any sand. Make sure that the clams are tightly closed (some may be slightly open but, if still alive, will close right up when tapped lightly). Discard any clams that remain open or appear broken. ❷ Place the clams in a large bowl of cold water and sprinkle the cornmeal over the water. Let the clams sit for about 30 minutes. Drain and rinse the clams once again to remove any cornmeal. ❸ Heat the oil in a large Dutch oven over medium heat. Add the shallots and sauté for 2 to 3 minutes, or until just softened. Add the tomatoes, white wine, garlic purée, parsley, 1 tablespoon chives, salt, and black pepper and bring to a simmer. Cook for 2 minutes and then stir in the red pepper flakes. ❹ Add the clams to the simmering liquid and cover tightly. Steam for 6 to 8 minutes, or until the clams open, sliding the pan back and forth over the burner every now and again to ensure the clams cook evenly. ❺ Remove the clams from the pan with a slotted spoon and place in a large soup tureen or individual shallow soup bowls. (Discard any that did not open.) Spoon the tomato liquid over the clams, garnish with the chives, and serve immediately.

[SERVES 4 ➡ 6]

4 pounds clams

1 tablespoon cornmeal

2 tablespoons olive oil

2 shallots, finely chopped

3 tomatoes, peeled, seeded, and finely diced

1 cup dry white wine

2 tablespoons Roasted Garlic Purée (page 175)

1 tablespoon finely chopped parsley

1 tablespoon finely chopped chives

salt and freshly ground black pepper

pinch of crushed red pepper flakes

finely chopped chives, for garnish

cornmeal-crusted soft-shell crabs with lemon-caper sauce

A specialty of Maryland, soft-shell crabs are in season from about May through August. The name actually refers to a growth stage of the crab (most commonly the blue crab found along the Atlantic and Gulf states), during which time it casts off its shell to grow a larger one. The entire crab can be eaten in its soft-shell state, and it is a simple delicacy when prepared with a few flavorful items. During their short season, the shellfish are air-freighted around the country, and are well worth the splurge to buy them fresh.

The best way to enjoy soft-shell crabs is to sauté them in butter, along with lemon juice, garlic, and capers—just enough ingredients to complement the crab without masking its inherent flavor. Serve them with Braised Spinach (page 125) and Roasted New Potatoes with Leeks (page 133).

8 soft-shell crabs

Cornmeal Coating
3 tablespoons all-purpose flour
3 tablespoons yellow cornmeal
pinch of cayenne pepper
salt and freshly ground black pepper

¼ cup unsalted butter
¼ cup olive oil
2 shallots, finely chopped
¼ cup fresh lemon juice
2 garlic cloves, minced
1 tablespoon capers, rinsed and drained
2 tablespoons finely chopped parsley
salt and freshly ground black pepper
lemon wedges, for garnish

❶ Remove the feelers underneath the crab shells on both sides. Rinse the crabs thoroughly and dry completely. ❷ Prepare the coating: Combine all the ingredients in a dish and stir to mix well. ❸ Heat 2 tablespoons of the butter and all of the olive oil in a very large skillet over medium-high heat. Add the shallots and sauté for 1 minute. ❹ Roll the crabs in the flour mixture and place them in the skillet. Sauté, turning once and shaking the pan to prevent the shallots from burning, for about 3 minutes on each side, or until the crabs have turned pink and are cooked through. Add the remaining 2 tablespoons butter, the lemon juice, garlic, capers, parsley, salt and pepper and cook for another 1 to 2 minutes, turning the crabs to coat them with the sauce. Taste for seasoning. ❺ To serve, arrange the crabs on a warmed serving platter or individual plates and garnish with lemon wedges. Serve immediately.

[SERVES 4]

crab cakes with citrus-mint salsa

These crab cakes are for true crab lovers, since they are full of the sweet meat of the Dungeness crab, with only a tiny bit of bread crumbs for binding. Panko flakes, Japanese-style bread crumbs, are used here for a crispy coating. To change the color of the vibrant salsa from orange to crimson, use blood oranges in place of regular oranges. Since blood oranges flourish in dry environments, they are grown primarily in California and Arizona. Harvesting in the West runs from December to May, although availability in eastern states is short-lived. Begin with Wilted Greens with Grilled Portobello Mushrooms and Dried Cherry Vinaigrette (page 49) and serve a big basket of Shoestring Potatoes (page 136) with the crab cakes.

❶ Prepare the crab cakes: In a large bowl, combine the egg, mayonnaise, mustard, and chives. Add the crab meat and fresh bread crumbs and mix well. Add the salt and cayenne pepper. ❷ Spread the panko on a baking sheet. Divide the crab mixture into 8 equal portions. Shape each portion into a cake about 2 inches in diameter and ¾ inch thick. Coat the crab cakes completely with the panko and, using a spatula, transfer them to another baking pan. Cover with plastic wrap and refrigerate for at least 1 hour or for up to 6 hours. ❸ Meanwhile, prepare the salsa: Place the sesame seeds in a small skillet over medium heat and toss for 1 to 2 minutes, or until lightly browned. Pour into a small dish and reserve. ❹ In a bowl, whisk together the scallions, orange zest, orange juice, lemon juice, olive oil, sesame oil, and ginger. Peel the grapefruits, removing all the white pith. Using a sharp knife, cut along both sides of each segment to release it from the membrane. Remove any seeds, then cut the segments into thirds. Repeat the method for the orange. Add the segments to the scallion mixture, along with the mint and sesame seeds. Mix well and season with the salt and pepper. Cover and refrigerate. ❺ Heat 1 tablespoon of the butter and 1 tablespoon of the olive oil in a large skillet over medium-high heat. Add half of the crab cakes and sauté, turning once with a spatula for about 4 minutes on each side, or until golden brown on both sides. Repeat with remaining butter, oil, and crab cakes. ❻ Transfer the crab cakes to individual plates and top with the salsa. Serve immediately.

Advance Preparation: Can be made up to 6 hours ahead through step 3, covered, and refrigerated.

[SERVES 4]

Crab Cakes

1 large egg, lightly beaten
1 tablespoon mayonnaise
1 teaspoon Dijon mustard
1 tablespoon finely chopped chives
1 pound cooked Dungeness crab meat,
    pulled apart into ½-inch chunks
½ cup fresh bread crumbs
salt
pinch cayenne pepper
½ cup panko (Japanese-style bread
    crumbs)

Citrus-Mint Salsa

1 teaspoon sesame seeds
2 scallions, white and light green parts
    only, thinly sliced
1 tablespoon finely chopped orange zest
1 tablespoon orange juice
1 tablespoon fresh lemon juice
1 tablespoon olive oil
2 drops dark sesame oil
½ teaspoon minced fresh ginger
2 pink grapefruits
1 orange
2 tablespoons finely chopped fresh mint
salt and freshly ground black pepper

2 tablespoons unsalted butter, for frying
2 tablespoons olive oil, for frying

grilled shrimp with ginger-coconut sauce

Thai restaurants have brought new, fresh flavor combinations to America's culinary scene. In this recipe, shrimp gets a Thai accent when marinated in lime, ginger, and cilantro and then threaded onto skewers for grilling. The shrimp are basted with the marinade during grilling, causing them to become wonderfully caramelized. Serve the shellfish over Herbed Vegetable Rice (page 113), and spoon the lime, ginger, and coconut sauce over the top. The tart, sweet sauce is supposed to be thin so that it flavors both the shrimp and rice underneath. Quickly sautéed snow peas or sugar snap peas make a nice accompaniment.

Marinade

½ cup fresh lime juice

1 tablespoon minced fresh ginger

2 shallots, finely chopped

2 tablespoons finely chopped cilantro

2½ tablespoons lemon or lime marmalade

⅛ teaspoon crushed red pepper flakes

⅓ cup olive oil

salt and freshly ground black pepper

1½ pounds large shrimp (4 to 6 per
    person), peeled and deveined with
    tails left on

Ginger-Coconut Sauce

1 tablespoon olive oil

1 tablespoon minced fresh ginger

2 shallots, finely chopped

juice of 1 lime

¾ cup coconut milk

6 tablespoons chicken stock

2 tablespoons unsalted butter, cut into
    6 equal pieces

Garnish

3 tablespoons finely chopped parsley

3 limes, halved

❶ Prepare the marinade: In a nonaluminum bowl, whisk together the lime juice, ginger, shallots, cilantro, marmalade, and pepper flakes. ❷ Slowly add the olive oil, whisking until incorporated. Add the salt and pepper and taste for seasoning. Add the shrimp to the marinade and toss to coat evenly. Cover and refrigerate for 30 minutes to 2 hours. ❸ Prepare the sauce: In a small saucepan, heat the oil over medium heat. Add the ginger and shallots and sauté for about 2 minutes, or until tender. Add the lime juice, coconut milk, and stock. Bring to a simmer and reduce, stirring occasionally for 3 to 5 minutes, or until thickened slightly. ❹ Pour the sauce through a strainer into a clean saucepan. Whisk in the butter over low heat, remove from the heat, and cover to keep warm. ❺ Meanwhile, prepare charcoal or gas grill for medium-high-heat grilling about 3 inches from the fire. Remove the shrimp from the marinade. Thread the shrimp onto 6 metal or bamboo skewers (soak bamboo in cold water for 30 minutes before grilling), and place the skewered shrimp flat on the grill. Grill, turning once and brushing each side with the marinade, for about 3 minutes on each side, or until cooked through. ❻ To serve, arrange the skewers on serving plates and spoon the warm sauce over them. Garnish with the parsley and lime halves.

Advance Preparation: Can be prepared up to 2 hours ahead through step 2.

[SERVES 6 ➡ 8]

shrimp-corn risotto

Reserving the shrimp shells and corn cobs to make a quick stock imparts extra flavor to this creamy dish. The seafood is enhanced by the presence of sweet corn, and the summery character of the dish can be taken one step further with the addition of halved cherry tomatoes. For an even more velvety consistency, stir in 1 to 2 tablespoons cream before serving. Arborio rice is essential to the creamy and slightly al dente consistency of this classic risotto. Other Italian rices that work well include Carnaroli and Vialone Nano. Additional tips for making successful risotto include using a heavy pot with a solid handle that feels comfortable in the hand, and a wooden spoon for stirring.

1 pound medium shrimp, peeled and
deveined, shells reserved

1 cup corn kernels (about 2 ears of corn,
cobs reserved)

6 cups water

5 sprigs fresh thyme

5 black peppercorns

about 2 cups chicken stock

3 tablespoons olive oil

1 small onion, finely chopped

1½ cups Arborio rice

¾ cup dry white wine

2 garlic cloves, minced

2 tablespoons finely chopped parsley

1 tablespoon finely chopped fresh dill

1 tablespoon finely chopped chives

salt and freshly ground black pepper

❶ Place the reserved shrimp shells and corn cobs in a saucepan with the water, and add the thyme and peppercorns. Bring to a boil over high heat, reduce the heat to medium, and simmer for 35 to 45 minutes, or until reduced by half. ❷ Strain the stock into a large liquid measuring cup (you should have 3 cups). Add enough chicken stock to make a total of 5 cups stock. Pour the stock into a saucepan over medium heat and bring to a simmer. ❸ Meanwhile, in another saucepan, heat 2 tablespoons of the oil over medium heat. Add the onion and sauté for 3 to 5 minutes, or until softened. Add the rice and stir for 1 minute, making sure all the grains are coated with the oil. Pour in ½ cup of the wine and stir, using a wooden spoon, until all of the liquid has been absorbed. Begin adding the stock ½ cup at a time, making sure the rice has absorbed the previous stock and always stirring to prevent sticking. The rice should begin to get creamy as you continue to add the stock and stir. ❹ Just before completing the risotto, after 25 to 30 minutes, cook the shrimp. In a large sauté pan, heat the remaining 1 tablespoon of olive oil over medium-high heat. Add shrimp and cook for 1 minute. Flip the shrimp, add the remaining ¼ cup wine and the garlic, and sauté for another 2 minutes, or until cooked through. ❺ Add the last ½ cup stock with the corn to the rice. Cook, stirring, until the stock is absorbed, 1 to 2 minutes. Turn off the heat, add the cooked shrimp, parsley, dill, and chives and stir gently to distribute evenly. Season with salt and pepper. Serve immediately in shallow bowls.

[SERVES 6]

Poultry

lemon-rosemary roasted chicken

Restaurants built around serving rotisserie chicken are wildly popular all over the country, which suggests that Americans love golden brown, crispy roasted chicken. This simple main course bird is also ideal for making sandwiches, salads, and pastas. Prepare the chicken in advance so that it is cool enough to slice for your lunch or picnic fare.

Marinade

1 tablespoon coarsely chopped
    fresh rosemary
3 garlic cloves, minced
¼ cup fresh lemon juice
¼ cup olive oil
⅛ teaspoon cayenne pepper
salt

1 frying chicken, 3½ pounds, split
6 sprigs fresh rosemary
6 sprigs fresh thyme
salt and freshly ground black pepper
1 cup water
fresh rosemary and thyme sprigs, for garnish

❶ Prepare the marinade: In large bowl, combine all the marinade ingredients and whisk to mix well. Taste for seasoning. Scoop out and reserve 3 tablespoons of the marinade for basting the chicken. ❷ Using the flat side of a heavy cleaver, flatten chicken halves by pounding very hard a few times. Slide your hand under the skin of the chicken breast and gently loosen it from the meat. Slip the sprigs of rosemary and thyme beneath the skin. Place the chicken in the bowl with the marinade and rotate the halves until they are completely coated. Cover and refrigerate for 2 to 4 hours. ❸ Preheat the oven to 425 degrees F. Remove the chicken from the marinade and place breast side up in a heavy, large roasting pan fitted with a rack. Sprinkle the chicken with salt and pepper and pour the water into the pan to keep the pan from burning as the marinade drips from the chicken. Roast the chicken, basting a few times with the reserved marinade mixture, for 45 to 50 minutes, or until golden brown and the juices run clear when a thigh is pierced with a knife. You may need to add more water to bottom of pan if it begins to burn. ❹ Transfer the chicken to a serving platter and arrange sprigs of rosemary and thyme around the edges. Carve and serve.

Advance Preparation: Can be prepared up to 1 day ahead, covered, refrigerated, and served chilled.

[SERVES 4]

twice-cooked barbecued chicken

My dear friend Connie Engel came up with this way of barbecuing chicken for entertaining to avoid the last-minute hassles of long cooking times. The chicken is first marinated and then cooked, or almost steamed, in an aromatic barbecue sauce. Finally, right before serving, it is barbecued so the skin becomes crisp and dark brown. Cooking it in this fashion keeps the bird moist on the inside and golden brown on the outside. Serve with Green Bean, Sweet Pepper, and Jicama Salad (page 53). Herbed Garlic Cheese Bread makes a nice addition (page 27).

❶ Prepare the marinade: In a small bowl, combine all the marinade ingredients and whisk to mix well. Taste for seasoning. Arrange the chicken pieces in a large, shallow nonaluminum dish and pour the marinade evenly over them. Turn the pieces to coat evenly. Cover and refrigerate for 2 to 4 hours, turning several times to make sure the marinade covers all the chicken. ❷ Preheat the oven to 375 degrees F. Remove the chicken from the marinade and pour off the marinade into a small saucepan. Place the chicken in a roasting pan large enough to hold the pieces in a single layer without crowding. Cover the pan very tightly with aluminum foil, and bake for about 35 minutes, or until the juices run clear when a thigh is pierced with a knife. Remove from the oven. ❸ Add the juices from the roasting pan to the marinade in the saucepan and place over medium-high heat. Bring to a boil and boil for 7 to 10 minutes, or until the marinade is reduced to a glaze. ❹ Prepare a charcoal or gas grill for medium-high-heat grilling about 3 inches from the fire. Place the chicken on the grill rack and grill, basting with the glaze and turning once, for 10 to 15 minutes, or until the skin is very crisp and brown. Transfer to a platter or individual plates and serve immediately.

Advance Preparation: Can be prepared up to 6 hours ahead through step 3, covered, and refrigerated. Remove the chicken from the refrigerator 30 minutes before grilling. The sauce may be refrigerated and then reheated just before grilling.

[SERVES 6 ➡ 8]

Marinade

¾ cup fresh orange juice

¼ cup red wine

¼ cup soy sauce

2 shallots, finely chopped

1 tablespoon Dijon mustard

⅓ cup bottled chili sauce

1 tablespoon dark molasses

salt and freshly ground black pepper

2 frying chickens, 3½ pounds each, cut up

grilled lime-cilantro chicken
with tomatillo salsa

This simple Southwest-style grilled chicken tastes great with Spicy Black Beans with Island Salsa (page 118) or Corn Salad with Cherry Tomatoes (page 55). Begin with American Bistro Caesar Salad with Roasted Garlic Dressing (page 50) and cap off the meal with Peach and Plum Crostata (page 141).

Marinade

¼ cup olive oil

¼ cup fresh lime juice

2 tablespoons finely chopped cilantro

1 tablespoon honey

1 shallot, finely chopped

½ teaspoon ground cumin

1 teaspoon finely chopped lime zest

salt and freshly ground black pepper

3 large whole chicken breasts,
   halved and boned

1 cup Tomatillo Salsa (page 183)

❶ Prepare the marinade: In a small bowl, combine all the marinade ingredients and whisk to mix well. Taste for seasoning. ❷ Place the chicken breasts between 2 sheets of plastic wrap and pound to flatten slightly with a meat pounder or the flat side of a cleaver. Arrange the chicken breasts in a large, shallow nonaluminum dish and pour the marinade evenly over them. Turn the pieces to coat evenly. Cover and refrigerate for 2 to 4 hours, turning several times to make sure the marinade covers all the chicken. ❸ Prepare a charcoal or gas grill for medium-high-heat grilling about 3 inches from the fire. Remove the chicken from the marinade and place on the grill rack. Grill, turning once, for 7 to 10 minutes on each side, or until the juices run clear when the meat is pierced with a knife. ❹ To serve, place the chicken on individual plates and spoon the salsa over the top.

Advance Preparation: Can be prepared up to 4 hours ahead through step 1. The salsa can be prepared up to 3 days ahead, covered, and refrigerated.

[SERVES 4 ➡ 6]

grilled citrus chicken with *raita* sauce

While experimenting with Indian foods, I have gained an appreciation for cooling *raitas*, yogurt sauces flavored with fruits or vegetables that provide relief from spicier dishes. In this recipe, chicken gently marinates in an herbed yogurt sauce to flavor and tenderize the chicken breasts, an ideal lowfat summer preparation since no oil is used. The dish may be served hot or at room temperature, but either way spoon a dollop of cucumber yogurt *raita* over each breast just before serving. Try serving these with Herbed Vegetable Rice (page 113) and Garden Vegetable Sauté (page 127).

❶ Make the marinade and sauce: In a large nonaluminum bowl, combine the yogurt, garlic, lime juice, cilantro, cumin, salt, and pepper, and whisk to mix well. Taste for seasoning. Scoop out 1 cup of the marinade, place in a separate bowl, add the cucumbers, cover, and refrigerate to use as the sauce. ❷ Place the chicken breasts between 2 sheets of plastic wrap and pound to flatten slightly with a meat pounder or the flat side of a cleaver. Place the flattened breasts in the bowl with the yogurt marinade and turn to coat evenly. Cover and refrigerate for at least 4 hours and up to 12, turning occasionally. ❸ Prepare a charcoal or gas grill for medium-high-heat grilling about 3 inches from the fire. Remove the chicken from marinade and place on the grill rack. Grill, turning once, for 7 to 10 minutes on each side, or until the juices run clear when the meat is pierced with a knife. ❺ To serve, place the chicken on a serving platter and garnish with lime slices and cilantro sprigs. Pass the reserved cucumber-yogurt sauce.

Advance Preparation: The marinade and sauce can be prepared up to 1 day ahead, covered, and refrigerated.

[SERVES 6]

Marinade and Sauce

2 cups low-fat plain yogurt

3 garlic cloves, minced

2 tablespoons fresh lime juice

2 tablespoons finely chopped cilantro

½ teaspoon ground cumin

salt and white pepper

2 pickling cucumbers, unpeeled,
    finely diced

3 whole chicken breasts, halved,
    skinned, and boned

Garnish

lime slices

cilantro sprigs

chicken pot pie with parmesan-cheddar crust

Rather than make individual pot pies in ceramic crocks, I make a single large pie in a casserole dish for an old-fashioned one-dish meal. A tender, flaky crust with hints of Parmesan and Cheddar covers the entire dish, enclosing the wonderful filling. Chunks of chicken breast and colorful diced vegetables meld together in a rich sauce flavored with sautéed leeks. Begin with a simple green salad, and for dessert try Ultimate Ice Cream Sundae (page 155).

2 large whole chicken breasts, skinned
    and boned
3½ cups chicken stock

Pastry
2 cups all-purpose flour
7 tablespoons freshly grated
    Parmesan cheese
½ cup shredded sharp Cheddar cheese
¾ cup chilled unsalted butter,
    cut into small pieces
½ cup ice water

Filling
3 medium carrots or 10 ounces
    baby carrots, peeled and cubed
3 red or tan thin-skinned potatoes,
    about ¾ pound total, cut into
    ½-inch pieces
3 stalks celery, sliced into
    1½-inch-thick pieces
4 tablespoons olive oil
½ pound portobello mushrooms
    (2 mushrooms), cut into large dice
4 leeks, white and light green parts only,
    cleaned and finely chopped
1 cup corn kernels, fresh (about 2 ears of
    corn) or thawed frozen
1 cup cooked fresh baby peas or thawed
    frozen petite peas

❶ In a saucepan combine 3 cups of the chicken stock and the water and bring to a simmer over medium heat. There should be enough liquid to cover the chicken. Add the chicken and simmer for 12 to 15 minutes, or until just cooked through when pierced with a knife. Remove from the heat and let the chicken cool in the liquid, then remove to a cutting board. Strain the chicken stock and set aside to use for the sauce and the leeks (there should be about 2½ cups stock). Cut the chicken into 1½ inch chunks. Set aside. ❷ Prepare the pastry: Combine the flour, both cheeses, the butter, and the ice water in a food processor fitted with the metal blade. Process until a crumblike texture forms. Gather the pastry together into a ball, kneading lightly until just combined. Wrap and refrigerate until ready to roll out. ❸ Prepare the filling: Bring a saucepan of water to a boil, add the carrots and potatoes, and cook for 7 minutes, or until slightly softened. Add the celery and cook for another 2 minutes, or until slightly softened. Drain well and place the cooked vegetables in a large bowl. ❹ In a skillet, heat 1 tablespoon of the olive oil over medium heat. Add the mushrooms and sauté for about 3 to 5 minutes, or until softened. Add to the cooked vegetables. Rinse and dry the skillet. Heat the remaining 3 tablespoons olive oil in the skillet over medium heat. Add the leeks and sauté for 10 to 12 minutes, or until very soft. Add half of the leeks to the cooked vegetables along with the corn, peas, and chicken pieces. ❺ Combine the remaining leeks and ½ cup of the reserved chicken stock in a blender and purée for about 2 minutes, or until silky smooth. Reserve. ❻ Melt the butter in a large saucepan over medium heat. Sprinkle in the flour and cook, stirring constantly, for 3 minutes. Slowly add the remaining reserved chicken stock, the half-and-half, salt, and pepper, and whisk the sauce for 5 to 7 minutes, or until it is smooth and thickened. Add the puréed leeks and the parsley, chives, and dill. Stir to combine and add the sauce to the cooked vegetable mixture.

Taste for seasoning. ❼ Preheat the oven to 400 degrees F. Grease a deep 9-by-13-inch baking dish with butter. Pour the vegetable-chicken mixture into the prepared dish. ❽ On a lightly floured surface, roll out the chilled dough into a 9-by-13-inch rectangle to fit the top of the dish. Crimp the edges decoratively. Brush the top and edges with the beaten egg. Cut 3 diagonal slits in the crust. Sprinkle the remaining tablespoon of Parmesan evenly over the top. Place the baking dish on a baking sheet. ❾ Bake the pie for 25 to 30 minutes, or until the crust is browned, checking the last few minutes to make sure it does not burn. (If the crust is browning too quickly, cover the dish with aluminum foil for the last few minutes of baking.) Serve immediately.

Advance Preparation: Can be made up to 1 day ahead through step 8, covered, and refrigerated. It can also be baked ahead, covered, refrigerated, then brought to room temperature and gently reheated in an oven at 325 degrees F for 20 minutes, or until bubbly hot.

[SERVES 6]

6 tablespoons unsalted butter
7 tablespoons all-purpose flour
1 cup half-and-half
salt and freshly ground black pepper
¼ cup finely chopped parsley
3 tablespoons finely chopped chives
1 tablespoon finely chopped fresh dill

1 large egg, lightly beaten,
    for brushing crust
1 tablespoon freshly grated Parmesan cheese

roasted cornish hens with
orange-honey-mustard glaze

America's favorite ballpark mustards have given way to a growing industry of specialty mustards from Arizona, Santa Barbara, California, and the Napa Valley. Some of these gourmet varieties are even celebrated with a weekend devoted to tastings of the nation's finest products.

Combining grainy and Dijon mustards gives this glaze an intense mustard flavor without overpowering it. Try experimenting with different types and brands to discover which ones work best in this zesty marinade. Orange juice and honey add a touch of sweetness. The same glaze is also good with pork tenderloin or boneless, skinless chicken breasts cut into 1-inch pieces and skewered for brochettes.

❶ Prepare the marinade and glaze: In a large nonaluminum bowl, combine all the ingredients, and whisk to mix well. Taste for seasoning. ❷ Carefully separate the skin from the hens by slipping your fingers gently under the skin and loosening it, yet keeping it attached to the birds. (You may need to wear gloves if you have long nails.) Place the hens in the bowl with the marinade. Massage the marinade underneath the skin, being careful not to tear the skins. Rotate the hens until they are completely covered with the marinade. Cover and refrigerate for 2 to 4 hours. ❸ Preheat the oven to 425 degrees F. Line a large jelly-roll pan or roasting pan with aluminum foil. Remove the hens from the marinade and place them in the lined pan. ❹ Roast the hens, basting with the pan juices every 15 minutes, for 40 to 45 minutes, or until the juices run clear when a thigh is pierced and the skin is golden brown. ❺ Place the hens on a serving platter or individual plates and garnish with the orange slices.

Advance Preparation: Can be prepared up to 4 hours ahead through step 2 and refrigerated. This is also good served cold on a luncheon buffet.

[SERVES 6]

Marinade and Glaze

1 cup fresh orange juice

1 teaspoon finely chopped orange zest

2 shallots, finely chopped

2 tablespoons honey

2 tablespoons Dijon mustard

1 tablespoon grainy mustard

1 tablespoon soy sauce

1 tablespoon balsamic vinegar

1 tablespoon olive oil

salt and freshly ground black pepper

6 Rock Cornish hens
orange slices, for garnish

soy-and-molasses-basted turkey breast with dried cranberry–apple compote

Roasting a boneless turkey breast eliminates much of the time and work involved with stuffing and carving a whole bird. The marinade turns the turkey a deep brown, and the gravy and compote add richness and sweetness to the meat. You can use sweetened dried cranberries (versus the regular dried cranberries) in the compote, but be sure to decrease the amount of brown sugar to taste.

If you would like to roast a whole bird, double the amount of the marinade, rub it all over the turkey and under the skin, and marinate the bird overnight. An unstuffed, 16-pound turkey should take about 4 hours to roast (add another hour for a stuffed turkey) at 325 degrees F, or until a thermometer inserted in the thickest part of the thigh registers 170 degrees F and the juices run clear. Proceed with the gravy and compote as described below. If you don't feel like having a traditional gravy, serve the skimmed juices from the turkey. Accompany the turkey breast with Butternut Squash and Carrot Purée with Ginger (page 128), or Perfect Mashed Potatoes (page 134), Garden Vegetable Sauté (page 127), and Pumpkin Ice Cream Pie with Gingersnap Crust (page 154).

Marinade

2 shallots, finely chopped
2 garlic cloves, minced
1 tablespoon balsamic vinegar
2 tablespoons soy sauce
2 tablespoons dark molasses
freshly ground black pepper
3 tablespoons olive oil

1 boned and tied turkey breast,
    about 3½ pounds
½ cup chicken stock

Dried Cranberry–Apple Compote

2 large Granny Smith or other tart green
    apples, peeled, cored, and finely
    chopped
½ cup dried cranberries
2 tablespoons brown sugar
1 tablespoon cider vinegar
⅛ teaspoon ground cinnamon
1 cup water

Gravy

½ cup unsalted butter
½ cup all-purpose flour
3½ cups turkey or chicken stock, heated
½ cup full-bodied red wine such as
    Merlot or Cabernet Sauvignon
salt and freshly ground black pepper

❶ Prepare the marinade: In a small bowl, whisk together the shallots, garlic, balsamic vinegar, soy sauce, molasses, and pepper. Slowly pour in the olive oil in a steady stream, whisking constantly until completely blended. Taste for seasoning. ❷ Place the turkey breast in a nonaluminum bowl and pour the marinade over the top. Turn the turkey to coat evenly, cover, and refrigerate for 3 to 4 hours. ❸ Position a rack in the lower-middle level of the oven and preheat to 325 degrees F. Transfer the turkey from the marinade to a roasting pan and pour any marinade in the bottom of the bowl over the turkey. Cover the pan with aluminum foil. Roast the turkey for 1½ hours. Remove the foil, brush the turkey with the marinade in the pan, pour in the ½ cup stock, and return the turkey to the oven. Roast for about 15 minutes longer, or until a meat thermometer inserted into the thickest part of the breast registers 170 degrees F, basting with the pan juices halfway through the cooking time. The skin should turn golden brown. ❹ Meanwhile, prepare the compote: In a small saucepan, combine the apples, cranberries, brown sugar, vinegar, cinnamon, and water over medium heat. Stir to mix well. Cover and cook, stirring occasionally, for 20 to 25 minutes, or until the apples begin to break down. (Adjust the sweetness by adding more brown sugar, if desired.) Remove from the heat, cover, and set aside. ❺ Remove the turkey breast from the roasting pan and place on a platter. Cover loosely with foil and let rest for 15 to 20 minutes before slicing.

❻ Pour the pan drippings into a gravy separator (or into a bowl and skim off the fat with a large spoon) and reserve. ❼ Prepare the gravy: In a large, heavy saucepan, melt the butter over medium heat, watching carefully so it does not burn. Add the flour slowly, whisking briskly until bubbles form. Continue whisking for 3 to 5 minutes, or until the mixture thickens and turns a golden brown. The color of this flour mixture, or roux, is important because it determines the final color of the gravy. ❽ Slowly pour in the warmed stock and the wine, whisking until completely blended. Continue cooking the gravy over medium heat for 15 to 20 minutes, or until it is thickened and no taste of flour remains. Pour in the reserved defatted pan drippings, whisking to incorporate completely. Add the salt and pepper and taste for seasoning. Pour into a gravy boat.

Advance Preparation: Can be prepared up to 4 hours ahead through step 2, covered, and refrigerated. The compote can be made up to 1 day ahead, covered, and refrigerated. Bring the compote to room temperature before serving.

[SERVES 6 ➡ 8]

stir-fried turkey and vegetables with avocado-corn salsa and warm corn tortillas

Turkey breast strips have caught on across the nation ever since the word came in that turkey is low fat and plenty tasty. Stir-frying strips of turkey breast along with colorful vegetables and Mexican spices is a quick technique that produces a pretty, fajitalike filling for warm corn or flour tortillas. This is a flexible dish since you can serve it rolled in flour tortillas for a quick family dinner, or open-face on corn tortillas for a Southwest party.

❶ Prepare the salsa: In a bowl, combine the tomatoes, corn, cilantro, parsley, jalapeño, lemon juice, salt, and pepper. Stir to mix well. Cover and refrigerate for 1 hour. After 1 hour, drain the salsa and spoon it into a serving bowl. Right before serving, add the avocado and taste for seasoning. ❷ Prepare the filling: In a large skillet with high sides or in a wok, heat 1 tablespoon of the oil over high heat, swirling to coat the sides. When the oil is hot, add the turkey strips and toss every 15 to 20 seconds for 3 to 4 minutes, or until the turkey is lightly browned and just cooked through. If using a wok, spread the turkey evenly around and up the sides of the pan so that the turkey comes into maximum contact with the heat. Remove to a side dish. ❸ Add the remaining 1 tablespoon oil to the pan over high heat, again swirling to coat the sides. Add the onion and toss for 1 minute. Add the bell pepper and jalapeño chile and toss every 15 to 20 seconds for 4 to 6 minutes, or until the onion is nicely softened. Add the garlic and tomato and cook another minute. Add the lime juice, cumin, cilantro, and reserved turkey strips, bring to a boil, and cook for 1 minute. Add the salt and pepper and taste for seasoning. ❹ Transfer to a serving bowl. Serve immediately with a basket of warm tortillas and small bowls of the sour cream and the salsa on the side. Garnish with the cilantro.

Advance Preparation: The salsa can be made up to 4 hours ahead, covered, and refrigerated.

[SERVES 4 ➡ 6]

Avocado-Corn Salsa

2 large tomatoes, peeled, seeded,
    and finely diced
½ cup corn kernels (about 1 ear of corn)
2 tablespoons finely chopped cilantro
2 tablespoons finely chopped parsley
1 jalapeño chile, seeded and minced
2 tablespoons fresh lemon juice
salt and freshly ground black pepper
1 avocado, pitted, peeled, and cut
    into ½-inch chunks

Filling

2 tablespoons vegetable or olive oil
1 pound turkey breast, cut into
    2-by-½-inch strips
1 red onion, thinly sliced
1 red bell pepper, seeded and cut into
    thin slices
1 jalapeño chile, seeded and minced
2 garlic cloves, minced
1 tomato, peeled and diced
3 tablespoons fresh lime juice
½ teaspoon ground cumin
2 tablespoons finely chopped cilantro
salt and freshly ground black pepper

Garnish

corn tortillas or flour tortillas, warmed
1 cup sour cream
cilantro leaves

crispy roasted duck
with black currant–plum sauce

The most common ducks found in the United States are Peking ducks, which are available fresh and frozen year-round. A common complaint with duck is the abundance of fat underneath the skin, but I have found several solutions to this problem. Steaming the duck prior to roasting produces moist, tender meat, and pricking the skin helps release some of the fat without causing the succulent bird to dry out.

This updated bistro classic is served in quarters rather than sliced for a more rustic presentation. A marinade of black currant syrup and plums lends a caramel coating to the skin, and doubles as a sauce to serve alongside the bird. Serve with Wild Rice Pilaf with Dried Fruits and Toasted Pine Nuts (page 116), and Garden Vegetable Sauté (page 127).

Marinade

½ pound dark-skinned plums, halved
*   and pitted*
3 tablespoons black currant syrup
½ cup port wine
1 cup fresh orange juice
¼ cup orange honey
1 teaspoon finely chopped orange zest
½ teaspoon ground allspice
salt and freshly ground black pepper

2 whole ducks, 4½ pounds each, neck and
*   giblets removed*
1 cup water
2 tablespoons unsalted butter
3 dark-skinned plums, pitted and
*   quartered, for garnish*

❶ Prepare the marinade: In a food processor fitted with the metal blade, combine all the ingredients and process until smooth. ❷ Place the ducks in a large nonaluminum bowl and pour the marinade evenly over them. Turn the ducks to coat them well. Cover and refrigerate for 2 to 4 hours, turning several times. ❸ Remove the ducks from the marinade and pat dry. Reserve the marinade (about 3 cups). Truss the duck with skewers by inserting one skewer in the thigh portion of the bird all the way through and out the other side. Do the same thing with the wing portion, being sure to go all the way through the bird and out the other side with each skewer. Using the tip of a small knife, gently prick the duck skin, particularly in fatty areas around the thighs and wings; be careful not to pierce the meat. ❹ Preheat the oven to 425 degrees F. In a small saucepan, bring the water to a boil. ❺ Place the ducks breast sides down on a rack in a large roasting pan. Pour the boiling water into the pan. Cover the ducks with a double layer of aluminum foil, crimping the foil along the edge of the pan to seal the ducks completely. Place the pan in the oven and steam the duck for 1 hour. ❻ Remove the pan from the oven, reduce the oven temperature to 400 degrees F, and slowly lift the foil from the pan, beginning with a corner to let the steam escape. Pour the pan drippings into a gravy separator (or into a bowl and skim off the fat with a large spoon) and reserve. ❼ Turn the ducks breast sides up on the rack, baste with 1 cup of the reserved marinade, return the pan to the oven, and roast for 25 to 30 minutes, or until the skin is a deep caramel color. ❽ Remove the roasted ducks from the oven and place on a cutting board. Cover loosely with foil while making the sauce. Drain off the drippings and add to the reserved drippings in the gravy separator (or defat with a spoon). In a small saucepan, combine the reserved marinade and drippings, and boil over high heat for 15 to 20 minutes, or until reduced to 1 cup. Skim off any fat, if necessary. Pour the reduced sauce through a fine-mesh strainer into a clean saucepan. Add the salt and pepper and taste for seasoning. Whisk in the butter piece by piece and keep the sauce warm. ❾ Quarter the ducks and place them on a serving platter or individual plates. Surround with the plum quarters and spoon the sauce over the ducks. Serve immediately.

Advance Preparation: Can be prepared up to 4 hours ahead through step 2.

[SERVES 4 ➡ 6]

Meats

ragout of beef with sun-dried tomatoes and winter vegetables

A handful of sun-dried tomatoes, natural thickeners packed with flavor, are added to this rich stew. Butternut squash and parsnips are quickly sautéed and stirred in at the last minute to keep their texture. Fresh herbs, red wine, and balsamic vinegar round out the depth of flavor. Serve with a simple green salad with Herb Vinaigrette (page 176) and a loaf of crusty bread to soak up the flavorful juices.

½ cup all-purpose flour

salt and freshly ground black pepper

3 pounds beef chuck, cut into 1½-inch
    cubes, patted dry

7 tablespoons olive oil

2 large onions, sliced

¼ cup balsamic vinegar

2 carrots, peeled and thinly sliced

4 garlic cloves, minced

1½ cups beef stock or veal stock

1 cup full-bodied red wine, such as Merlot
    or Cabernet Sauvignon

¼ cup tomato paste

4 sprigs parsley

2 sprigs fresh thyme or ¼ teaspoon dried

10 sun-dried tomatoes, soaked in boiling
    water for 20 minutes, drained
    and quartered

1 small butternut squash, about ½ pound,
    halved, seeded, peeled, and cut into
    ¾-inch chunks

3 parsnips, peeled and cut into ¾-inch
    chunks

1 cup chicken stock

¼ cup finely chopped parsley

❶ Place the flour, salt, and pepper in a large bowl or plastic bag. Thoroughly dredge the beef, then shake off any excess flour. ❷ In a large nonstick skillet, heat 3 tablespoons of the olive oil over medium-high heat. Add the beef pieces in batches, and brown evenly on all sides, for 5 to 7 minutes for each batch. Using a slotted spatula, transfer the beef pieces to a bowl and reserve. ❸ Add 2 more tablespoons oil to the pan, add the onions, and sauté over medium-high heat for 3 to 5 minutes, or until softened. Add the balsamic vinegar and continue sautéing for about 15 minutes, or until the onions are nicely browned and caramelized. Add the carrots and sauté for about 3 minutes longer, or until slightly tender. Add 3 of the garlic cloves and sauté for another minute. Add the stock, wine, tomato paste, parsley sprigs, thyme and sun-dried tomatoes, turn up the heat and bring to a boil. Return the meat to the sauce and reduce the heat to a low simmer. Cover and simmer, stirring occasionally, for about 2 hours, or until the meat is tender. Uncover, turn up the heat to medium, and simmer for about 15 minutes or until the sauce is slightly thickened. Taste for seasoning. ❹ A few minutes before serving, heat the remaining 2 tablespoons oil in a large skillet over medium heat. Add the squash and parsnips and sauté for 3 to 5 minutes, stirring frequently. Add the remaining 1 clove garlic and toss to coat, sautéing for 1 minute. Add the chicken stock, turn up the heat, cover, and cook for 5 to 7 more minutes, or until the squash and parsnips are fork tender. ❺ Remove the skillet from the heat and season the vegetables with the salt, pepper, and 2 tablespoons of the chopped parsley, mixing to combine. Taste for seasoning. Add to the beef and stir to mix. Spoon the stew into a large serving bowl or platter. Garnish with the remaining 2 tablespoons chopped parsley and serve.

Advance Preparation: Can be prepared up to 2 days ahead through step 3, covered, and refrigerated.

[SERVES 6]

braised short ribs with tomato barbecue sauce

Beef short ribs are one of the most flavorful cuts of beef, and long, slow cooking produces such tender meat it almost falls off the bone. It is also one of the fattier cuts of beef, so the challenge is to reduce the fat while still retaining the flavor. Skimming the braising liquid before serving removes any fat that is left. If you have time, cool and refrigerate the ribs and sauce (separately, covered) to make removing the fat even easier and to improve the flavor greatly. These ribs taste best with Perfect Mashed Potatoes (page 134).

❶ In a large bowl, season the ribs with the salt and pepper. ❷ Preheat the oven to 325 degrees F. In a 12-inch nonstick skillet, heat 2 tablespoons of the vegetable oil over medium-high heat. In batches, brown the ribs on all sides, using kitchen tongs to turn and brown them evenly, for 7 to 10 minutes. Remove the ribs with a slotted spoon, drain briefly on paper towels, and then place in a large, ovenproof Dutch oven or other heavy pot. ❸ In the same skillet, add the remaining 1 tablespoon oil, increase the heat to medium-high, and brown the onions for 7 to 10 minutes, stirring frequently and watching carefully so that they brown but do not burn. Add the carrots and sauté for another 2 to 3 minutes, or until softened. Add the garlic and cook for another minute. Add the tomatoes, barbecue sauce, beef stock, and mustard and stir well. Increase the heat to high and simmer for 1 minute to mix the flavors. Pour the tomato sauce mixture over the short ribs and mix to combine. ❹ Cover and bake the ribs for about 3 hours, or until the meat is very tender, turning the ribs every 45 minutes. Season with the salt and pepper and garnish with the parsley. Serve immediately.

Advance Preparation: Can be prepared up to 3 days ahead, covered, and refrigerated. Reheat gently on the stove top.

[SERVES 6]

5 pounds lean beef short ribs, cut into
    3- to 4-inch pieces
salt and freshly ground black pepper
3 tablespoons vegetable oil
2 onions, thickly sliced into rings
4 carrots, peeled and sliced into ½-inch-
    thick slices
4 garlic cloves, minced
1 cup crushed tomatoes
1 cup bottled barbecue sauce
1 cup beef stock
1 teaspoon Dijon mustard
2 tablespoons finely chopped parsley,
    for garnish

braised brisket of beef with onions and garlic

This is really a cross between mom's brisket and the best pot roast you've ever tasted. Inspired by Nach Waxman's recipe in *The New Basics* cookbook, this comforting potted beef braises tenderly and slowly in an onion, leek, and beer compote, the flavor heightened by the addition of sun-dried tomato paste and whole braised garlic cloves. The sun-dried tomato paste adds an extra punch of flavor, although regular tomato paste can be substituted. Make sure to pick a flavorful lager, but watch out for bitterness.

The key to this recipe is long, slow cooking. It prevents the meat from shrinking and preserves the sweet onion compote bed that helps to keep the beef moist and tender. Cutting the brisket halfway through the cooking process assures that each slice of meat will be evenly flavored with the sauce, and makes serving a snap. Offer Crispy Potato Pancakes (page 135), Cinnamon Spice Applesauce (page 186), and Roasted Seasonal Vegetables (page 123) as accompaniments.

3 tablespoons olive oil

1 first cut brisket, 4 to 5 pounds

salt and freshly ground black pepper

4 onions, thinly sliced

4 leeks, white and light green parts only,
*   cleaned and thinly sliced*

3 carrots, peeled and sliced

16 garlic cloves, peeled but left whole

1 cup lager beer

¼ cup sun-dried tomato paste

2 tablespoons finely chopped parsley,
*   for garnish*

❶ In a very large, heavy, deep ovenproof Dutch oven or similar pot, heat 2 tablespoons of the olive oil over medium-high heat. Meanwhile, dry the brisket well and season with salt and pepper on both sides. Brown the brisket for about 4 minutes on each side, or until nicely browned. (This will ensure that the sauce is a deep brown and has a rich flavor.) Remove the brisket to a large dish and reserve. ❷ Add the remaining 1 tablespoon oil to the pan over medium heat. Add the onions and leeks and sauté for 15 to 20 minutes, or until a rich, golden brown, scraping up the browned bits from the bottom of the pan as the onions cook. Add the carrots and garlic and cook for another 2 minutes. Add the beer, salt, and pepper. ❸ Preheat the oven to 375 degrees F. Arrange the brisket on top of the onion mixture in the pot and, using a rubber spatula, spread the sun-dried tomato paste evenly over the brisket to glaze evenly. Cover, place in the oven, and braise for 1½ hours. ❹ Remove the brisket to a carving board and slice the meat against the grain. Place the meat back in the pot, overlapping the slices. Return the pot to the oven and continue cooking the brisket for another 1½ to 2 hours, or until very tender when pierced with a fork. ❺ To serve, transfer the brisket slices to a serving dish with a rim to catch the sauce. Spoon the sauce over the slices and garnish with the parsley. Serve immediately.

Advance Preparation: Can be made up to 3 days ahead, covered, and refrigerated. Reheat at 350 degrees F for 30 minutes before serving.

[SERVES 6 ➡ 8]

grilled entrecôte

When I lived in Paris, one of my favorite dinner spots was a place that specialized in just one dish, entrecôte, which we know as the rib-eye. My favorite steak was grilled over vines and served "black and blue" (charred and blood rare). This is my adaptation of that taste memory.

These thick rib-eyes rely on a pungent marinade to bring out the rich flavor of the meat. Anchovies are the secret ingredient here, giving the steaks an intriguing taste. They are best served medium-rare, but adjust the grilling time and doneness to suit your taste. In the summer months, accompany the rib-eyes with Roasted Summer Tomatoes (page 122). White Bean Stew with Toasted Bread Crumbs (page 117) also makes a splendid accompaniment, especially for a more substantial cold-weather meal.

❶ Prepare the marinade: In a small bowl, combine all the ingredients and whisk to mix well. Taste for seasoning. Arrange the steaks in a large, shallow nonaluminum dish and pour the marinade evenly over the meat to coat well. Cover and refrigerate for at least 4 hours, or for up to overnight, turning several times to make sure the marinade covers all the meat. ❷ Remove the meat from the refrigerator 30 minutes before grilling. Prepare a charcoal or gas grill for medium-high-heat grilling about 3 inches from the fire. Grill the steaks, turning once, for 7 to 9 minutes on each side, or until medium-rare. The steaks should be almost charred on the outside and medium-rare on the inside. ❸ Place the steaks on a carving platter and let rest for 10 minutes. Slice the steaks against the grain into ½-inch-thick slices and serve immediately.

Advance Preparation: Can be made up to 12 hours ahead through step 1.

[SERVES 6 ➡ 8]

Marinade

2 garlic cloves, minced

2 shallots, minced

1 tablespoon finely chopped fresh thyme

1 tablespoon finely chopped chives

2 tablespoons finely chopped parsley

3 anchovy fillets, finely chopped

1 tablespoon finely chopped lemon zest

¾ cup olive oil

salt and freshly ground black pepper

3 rib-eye steaks with rib attached,
      about 1½ pounds each and
      2 inches thick

goat cheese–stuffed hamburgers
with two-olive spread

Nearly everyone has his or her own opinion as to what makes a great hamburger. Certainly it is the quality of the beef, but it is also other touches. Maybe it is using bottled chili sauce in the mix, or adding a touch of ice water to make the burgers really juicy. This Mediterranean-influenced burger gives cheeseburgers a whole new meaning. Fresh goat cheese, preferably an American-produced one, is tucked into the center of the burger so that the cheese melts as the meat cooks. Spooning Two-Olive Spread over the top completes this American bistro favorite, with no need for any other condiments.

2 pounds ground sirloin

1 tablespoon finely chopped fresh basil

3 ounces fresh goat cheese

6 kaiser rolls, split and lightly toasted

¾ cup Two-Olive Spread (page 22)

6 leaves lettuce such as romaine
or red-leaf

6 slices beefsteak tomato

❶ In a bowl, combine the ground sirloin and basil and mix well. Shape into 6 thick patties. ❷ Make a pocket in the center of each patty, fill each pocket with 1 tablespoon of the goat cheese, and cover with the meat. Press into patties ¾ inch thick. ❸ Heat a grill pan or sauté pan over medium-high heat. Spray lightly with nonstick cooking spray, and add the burgers. Cook for 3 to 4 minutes on the first side, flip, and cook 4 to 6 minutes on the second side for medium-rare, or until desired doneness. ❹ To serve, place the burgers on the toasted bun halves and top each burger with 2 tablespoons of the olive spread. Top with lettuce and tomato and finish with the top of the bun.

Advance Preparation: Can be made up to 4 hours ahead through step 2, covered, and refrigerated.

[SERVES 6]

southwestern-style beef chili

This hearty American classic borrows heavily from the pantries of Mexico and the Southwest by incorporating spices such as oregano, cumin, and cinnamon, and staples such as unsweetened chocolate in the style of a mole sauce. The chipotle chile casts a light smoky flavor with just a touch of heat. Look for chipotle chiles preserved in *adobo* sauce so that some of the sauce will also flavor the chili.

The small chunks of beef chuck become meltingly tender and the sautéed red peppers add a hint of sweet fruitiness. I like to serve this with warmed corn bread and a simple green salad tossed with Creamy Pumpkin Seed Dressing (page 47). It is a great recipe to make for a crowd because it is the quintessential one-dish meal and can be prepared completely ahead and reheated just before serving.

❶ In a 6-quart pot, heat 2 tablespoons of the oil over medium heat. In batches, brown the beef on all sides for 5 to 7 minutes, or until it is well browned. (Don't crowd the pan or the meat will steam.) Remove to a bowl and reserve. ❷ Add another 2 tablespoons oil to the pot over medium heat. Add the onions and sauté until softened and lightly browned. Add the jalapeño chile and sauté for another minute. Add the garlic, oregano, cumin, coriander, cinnamon, and chili powder; sauté, stirring constantly, for another 2 minutes, or until the spices have mixed together and there is an aroma in the air. ❸ Add the beer, stock, tomatoes and chipotle chile and bring to a low simmer. Return the meat to the pot. Cover partially and simmer over low heat, stirring occasionally, for 1½ hours, or until the meat is tender. ❹ Meanwhile, in a skillet, heat the remaining 2 tablespoons oil over medium heat. Add the red and yellow peppers and sauté for 3 to 5 minutes, or until cooked but slightly crisp. Set aside. ❺ Add the kidney and pinto beans to the chili mixture and continue simmering, uncovered, for 30 minutes longer, or until slightly thickened. ❻ Add the grated chocolate, sautéed peppers, salt, and pepper, and stir until the chocolate is melted. Taste for seasoning. Serve in large chili or pottery bowls. Surround with small bowls of sour cream, salsa, shredded Cheddar cheese, and chopped onions.

Advance Preparation: Can be prepared up to 3 days ahead, covered, and refrigerated. Remove from the refrigerator 1 hour before reheating. The chili can also be frozen for up to 1 month, thawed, and reheated gently. Adjust the seasonings.

MAKES 3 QUARTS [SERVES 10 ➡ 12]

6 tablespoons vegetable oil

3 pounds beef chuck, cut into ½-inch
    chunks, patted dry

3 large onions, finely chopped

1 jalapeño chile, seeded and finely chopped

8 garlic cloves, minced

4 teaspoons ground oregano

3 tablespoons ground cumin

2 teaspoons ground coriander

1 teaspoon ground cinnamon

½ cup chili powder

1 can (12 ounces) beer

2½ cups beef stock or veal stock

1 can (28 ounces) crushed tomatoes

1 canned chipotle in adobo, *chopped*

1 red bell pepper, seeded and cut into
    ½-inch dice

1 yellow bell pepper, seeded and cut into
    ½-inch dice

1 can (15-ounces) kidney beans

1 can (16-ounces) pinto beans ½ ounce
    (½ square) unsweetened chocolate,
    grated

salt and freshly ground black pepper

Garnish

sour cream

tomato salsa

shredded sharp Cheddar cheese

chopped scallion or red onion

grilled veal chops with fresh thyme

These grilled veal chops are the epitome of bistro cooking: simple, quick, and full of flavor. The lime marinade penetrates the thick chops so that they remain incredibly tender after grilling. Fresh herbs complement the delicate veal, making this is an ideal warm weather dish. The reason the chops are finished in the oven is because they tend to burn on the outside while the interior is still underdone. This is particularly true when the veal chops are very thick. Serve with Garden Vegetable Sauté (page 127) or Spinach-Carrot Terrine with Red Pepper–Tomato Sauce (page 130).

❶ Prepare the marinade: In a small bowl, combine all the ingredients and whisk to mix well. Taste for seasoning. ❷ Brush both sides of the veal chops with the marinade and place in a nonaluminum baking dish. Cover and refrigerate for 2 to 4 hours. ❸ Preheat the oven to 450 degrees F. Prepare a charcoal or gas grill for medium-high-heat grilling about 3 inches from the fire, or heat a grill pan over medium-high heat. Spray the grill pan with nonstick cooking spray. ❹ Season the veal chops with salt and pepper. Place on the grill and grill for about 7 minutes on each side. Quickly sear the edges all around, about 2 minutes. Transfer the veal chops to a roasting pan and finish cooking in the oven for 4 to 6 minutes more, or until the veal is still very pink inside. ❺ To serve, place the veal chops on serving plates and garnish with the thyme.

Advance Preparation: Can be prepared up to 4 hours ahead through step 2, covered, and refrigerated.

[SERVES 4]

Marinade

3 tablespoons olive oil
2 tablespoons fresh lime juice
1 shallot, finely chopped
1 tablespoon finely chopped fresh thyme
salt and freshly ground black pepper

4 veal rib chops, ¾ pound each and
*   1½ inches thick*
salt and freshly ground black pepper
finely chopped fresh thyme, for garnish

grilled veal sausages with sautéed apples and caramelized fennel and red onions

Designer sausages have become almost as American as hot dogs. Some of the varieties being produced by chefs and sausage makers across the country include turkey with sun-dried tomato or chicken with apple. Today, there is a sausage for almost every palate. For this recipe, I like a simple veal or chicken sausage because the sautéed apples and slightly sweet relish complement the milder flavors. If you prepare the Caramelized Fennel and Red Onions ahead of time, this an impressive last-minute dish.

2 tablespoons unsalted butter

2 Pippin or Granny Smith apples, peeled, cored, and cut into ¼-inch-thick slices

1 tablespoon fresh lemon juice

1 teaspoon finely chopped lemon zest

2 tablespoons water

12 cooked veal sausages, 2½ to 3 pounds total, sliced in half horizontally

½ cup Caramelized Fennel and Red Onions (page 185), heated

assorted mustards, for serving

❶ In a skillet, melt the butter over medium heat. Add the apple slices and sauté, stirring constantly to brown evenly for about 5 minutes, or until they are slightly softened. Add the lemon juice and zest and cook for another minute to combine. Add the water and deglaze the pan to glaze the apples, scraping up the browned bits. Keep warm. ❷ Prepare a charcoal or gas grill for medium-high-heat grilling, about 3 inches from the fire. Grill the sausages, turning as needed, for about 5 to 7 minutes, or until browned on all sides. ❸ To serve, arrange the sausages on individual plates and spoon some of the apple slices and Caramelized Fennel and Red Onions over each sausage. Serve your favorite variety of mustards on the side.

Advance Preparation: Can be made up to 1 hour ahead through step 1, and covered to keep warm. The Caramelized Fennel and Red Onions can be prepared up to 3 days ahead, covered, and refrigerated. Remove from the refrigerator 1 hour before serving.

[SERVES 6]

veal stew with tomatoes and shiitake mushrooms

Roasting the veal first, rather than sautéing, brings out its full flavor and lightly browns the meat. This take-off on veal Marengo adds dried shiitake mushrooms to the stew for an earthy touch. As the garlic cloves slowly simmer, they melt right into the sauce. Ask your butcher for veal shoulder meat, which retains its tender texture when slowly cooked. Serve the stew in deep pasta-style bowls on a bed of Pasta with Asparagus and Leeks (page 107). If you prefer to serve this with simple buttered noodles, you can add thawed frozen petite peas to the stew just before serving.

❶ Place the mushrooms in a bowl and add boiling water to cover. Soak for at least 20 minutes to soften, then drain, reserving the soaking liquid. Cut the mushrooms into 1-inch pieces. Reserve. ❷ Preheat the oven to 450 degrees F. In a large ovenproof roasting pan, combine the veal, salt, pepper, onions, and flour and toss together well, making sure that the flour evenly covers all of the ingredients. Place the pan in the oven for 20 minutes. After 10 minutes, using long oven mitts to protect your hands, quickly toss all the ingredients with a long-handled spoon. Add the garlic cloves, toss again to combine, and continue roasting for about 10 minutes longer, or until the garlic is lightly browned. ❸ Remove the roasting pan from the oven and transfer all the ingredients to a large Dutch oven or other heavy pot. Place the roasting pan on the stove top over medium heat and add the stock and ½ cup of the reserved mushroom soaking liquid, scraping up the browned bits. Add the tomatoes and juice, thyme, rosemary, and reserved mushrooms and mix to combine. Transfer the tomato mixture to the Dutch oven and place over medium heat. Bring the mixture to a simmer. Cover and simmer over low heat for 1¼ hours, or until the meat is tender, stirring once or twice to cook the meat evenly. ❹ If the sauce is too thick, add more of the mushroom soaking liquid to reach the desired consistency. Season with the salt and pepper and taste for seasoning. Spoon the stew into a large serving bowl or individual bowls, garnish with the parsley, and serve immediately.

Advance Preparation: Can be prepared up to 5 days ahead, covered and refrigerated. The stew can also be frozen for up to 1 month, thawed, and reheated gently. Adjust the seasonings.

[SERVES 4 ➡ 6]

1 ounce dried shiitake mushrooms

boiling water, as needed

3 pounds veal stew, cut into 2-inch cubes, patted dry

salt and freshly ground black pepper

2 onions, finely chopped

3 tablespoons all-purpose flour

20 garlic cloves, peeled but left whole

½ cup rich beef or veal stock

1 can (28 ounces) diced tomatoes, with juice

1 tablespoon finely chopped fresh thyme

1 tablespoon finely chopped fresh rosemary

¼ cup finely chopped parsley, for garnish

braised lamb shanks with merlot and prunes

Lamb shanks have come back into favor with their rich flavor and make-ahead feature. These tender morsels require slow braising, and moist California prunes add a slightly sweet counterpoint. Serve with Perfect Mashed Potatoes (page 134) flavored with white horseradish cream and Roasted Seasonal Vegetables (page 123).

6 lamb shanks, ¾ to 1 pound each,
    patted dry
all-purpose flour, for dusting
salt and freshly ground black pepper
¼ cup olive oil
2 carrots, peeled and finely chopped
1 onion, finely chopped
1 stalk celery, finely chopped
3 tablespoons finely chopped fresh basil
2 tablespoons finely chopped fresh thyme
4 garlic cloves, minced
2 cups chicken stock
2 cups Merlot wine or other full-bodied
    red wine
1 container (9 ounces) moist-packaged
    prunes, cut into bite-sized pieces
1 cup canned crushed tomatoes
3 tablespoons tomato paste
2 tablespoons finely chopped parsley,
    for garnish

❶ Preheat the oven to 325 degrees F. Place the flour, salt, and pepper in a large bowl. Dredge the lamb lightly, then shake off any excess flour. In a large Dutch oven, heat 2 tablespoons of the olive oil over medium-high heat. Add the lamb, in two batches, and brown on all sides, for about 8 minutes for each batch. Using tongs, transfer the lamb to a large roasting pan. ❷ Reduce the heat to medium and add the remaining 2 tablespoons olive oil to the Dutch oven. Add the carrots, onion, celery, basil, and thyme and sauté, stirring occasionally, for 6 to 8 minutes, or until the vegetables are tender. Add the garlic and cook for another minute. ❸ Stir in the stock, wine, prunes, crushed tomatoes, and tomato paste. Bring to a simmer. Pour the sauce over the lamb in the roasting pan and cover tightly with aluminum foil. Place in the oven and cook the lamb until the meat is very tender and beginning to fall off the bones, about 2 hours. (Adjust the cooking time for larger or smaller lamb shanks.) ❹ Transfer the lamb to a platter and tent it with foil to keep warm. Pour the pan juices into a saucepan and bring to a simmer over medium-high heat. Simmer for about 20 minutes, or until thickened and reduced by half. Taste for seasoning. ❺ Pour the reduced pan juices over the lamb. Garnish with the parsley and serve immediately.

Advance Preparation: Can be prepared up to 2 days ahead, covered, and refrigerated. Reheat gently.

[SERVES 6]

roasted rack of lamb with herbed crust

Rack of lamb need not be reserved for special occasions, especially when the preparation is as easy as this one. Coating the lamb with a mixture of bread crumbs, herbs and mustard gives the meat a crispy coating and adds flavor to each bite. *Demi-glace* is the secret to the velvety brown sauce, which can also be used as a sauce for Grilled Entrecôte (page 93). Serve the individual lamb chops with Braised Spinach (page 125) and Roasted New Potatoes with Leeks (page 133) for an impressive dinner.

Sauce

1 shallot, finely chopped

¼ cup full-bodied red wine, such as Merlot or Cabernet Sauvignon

¾ cup demi-glace

1½ teaspoons grainy mustard

1 teaspoon dark brown sugar

2 tablespoons unsalted butter

salt and freshly ground black pepper

2 racks of lamb, 8 chops or about 2½ pounds each, trimmed of excess fat and meat scraped off upper 1½ inches of each bone (frenched)

1 cup coarse fresh French bread crumbs

2 shallots, finely chopped

2 teaspoons grainy mustard

1 tablespoon finely chopped fresh basil

1 tablespoon finely chopped fresh thyme

2 tablespoons finely chopped parsley

salt and freshly ground black pepper

2 tablespoons olive oil

2 tablespoons chicken stock

fresh thyme leaves and parsley sprigs, for garnish

❶ Prepare the sauce: In a skillet, whisk together the shallot, red wine, *demi-glace*, 1 teaspoon of the mustard, and the sugar. Bring to a simmer over high heat and cook, stirring occasionally, for 5 to 7 minutes, or until the liquid is reduced by half. Remove from the heat and pour through a fine-mesh strainer into a clean small saucepan. Whisk in the butter and the remaining ½ teaspoon mustard. Season with salt and pepper and taste for seasoning; keep warm. ❷ Preheat the oven to 425 degrees F. Place the racks of lamb in a roasting pan, bone side down and roast for 20 to 25 minutes, depending on their size, for medium-rare. To test, insert an instant-read thermometer into the thickest part of the lamb; it should read 135 degrees F for medium-rare. Remove from the oven and let the lamb rest for 5 minutes. Drain off all the fat in the roasting pan. ❸ While the meat is roasting, in a small bowl, combine the bread crumbs, shallots, mustard, basil, thyme, parsley, salt, pepper, olive oil, and stock. Mix well. ❹ Preheat the broiler. Spread the bread crumb mixture evenly over the meat side of the racks. Place the racks under the broiler for 2 to 3 minutes, or until they are lightly browned. Be careful not to burn them. ❺ To serve, place the racks on a serving platter or carving board. Slice the chops by cutting between the bones. Spoon the sauce around the chops and garnish with additional herb sprigs. Serve 2 or 3 chops per person.

Advance Preparation: Can be prepared up to 1 hour ahead through step 1, covered, and kept at room temperature. Gently reheat the sauce.

[SERVES 4]

baked pork chops stuffed with apples and prunes

Double-thick pork chops are available at many markets, but if they're not displayed, ask your butcher to cut them for you. Have a 1-inch-wide incision cut horizontally on the loin part of the chop, making sure that it goes all the way through to the shin bone. That way there will be enough room to stuff the chop.

This stuffing is perfectly suited to pork with its slightly sweet accents of fresh apples and dried prunes and a touch of dried sage. The sauce is very easy to prepare and adds an extra layer of flavor. Don't worry if some of the stuffing comes out during baking, as it adds extra flavor and texture to the sauce. Serve with Roasted New Potatoes with Leeks (page 133) and steamed green beans.

❶ Prepare the stuffing: In a skillet, heat the olive oil over medium heat. Add the onions and sauté for 3 to 5 minutes, or until softened. Add the apple and sauté for about 3 minutes more, or until almost tender. Add the garlic and sauté for another minute. Remove from the heat. In a bowl, combine the onion-apple mixture with the sage, bread crumbs, prunes, salt, pepper, and apple cider, stirring to mix well. Taste for seasoning. ❷ Fill the pockets in the pork chops with the stuffing and secure each opening with toothpicks if the slit is larger than 1 inch wide. ❸ Preheat the oven to 375 degrees F. In a large nonstick skillet, heat the oil over medium-high heat. Using kitchen tongs, brown the pork chops for 3 to 4 minutes on each side, or until golden brown. (Push the toothpicks down when turning over.) Carefully transfer the pork chops to a roasting pan that will hold the chops close together in one layer. Reserve the skillet. ❹ Pour ¾ cup of the apple cider around the chops. Cover with aluminum foil and bake for 15 minutes. Remove the foil and finish baking for another 10 to 20 minutes, depending on how thick the pork chops are, or until they are well browned and cooked through. Insert an instant-read thermometer into the thickest part of the meat; it should read 150 degrees F (the pork will continue to cook). ❺ Carefully transfer the pork chops to a heated serving platter and cover with foil. Pour the juices from the roasting pan into the reserved skillet. Add the stock and the remaining ½ cup apple cider and place over medium-high heat. Deglaze the skillet by scraping up the browned bits, then cook for about 5 minutes, or until the liquid is reduced by one-third. Add the cream and swirl thoroughly into the sauce. Simmer for about 3 minutes more, or until the sauce thickens slightly and will coat the back of a spoon. Season with salt and pepper. Spoon the sauce over the pork chops, garnish with parsley, and serve immediately.

Advance Preparation: The stuffing can be prepared up to 1 day ahead, covered, and refrigerated. Bring to room temperature before proceeding with recipe.

Stuffing

3 tablespoons olive oil

1 small onion, finely chopped

1 small green apple, peeled, cored, and finely chopped

2 garlic cloves, minced

¼ teaspoon ground dried sage

1 cup fine dried bread crumbs

5 pitted moist-packaged prunes, cut into eighths

salt and freshly ground black pepper

2 tablespoons apple cider

4 double-thick pork loin chops, slit horizontally with a 1-inch pocket almost to the bone (see recipe introduction)

1¼ cups apple cider

½ cup rich beef stock

2 tablespoons whipping cream

salt and freshly ground black pepper

2 tablespoons finely chopped parsley, for garnish

Pasta, Polenta, Grains, and Legumes

baked penne with eggplant, chicken, and smoked mozzarella

Penne pasta has joined the ranks of macaroni as one of America's top comfort foods, and it has woven its way into our American bistro menus. This Italian-influenced dish combines rustic roasted vegetables with Tomato-Herb Sauce (page 181) and smoked mozzarella. For an even more complex flavor, add other vegetables such as roasted bell peppers.

I particularly like this as a party dish since it can be assembled completely ahead of time and then baked at the last moment. For a simple buffet, serve with American Bistro Caesar Salad with Roasted Garlic Dressing (page 50) and Herbed Garlic Cheese Bread (page 27), and, for dessert, Winter Apple Crisp with Dried Fruits (page 143). For another variation, omit the chicken and pair the pasta with Lemon-Rosemary Roasted Chicken (page 74), sliced roasted leg of lamb, or tenderloin of beef.

3 cups chicken stock or water

2 whole chicken breasts, boned

2 tablespoons olive oil

2 leeks, white and light green parts only,
    cleaned and coarsely chopped

5 zucchini, cut into 1-inch-thick slices

2 eggplants, cut into ¾-inch chunks

salt and freshly ground black pepper

1 pound dried penne rigati

4 cups Tomato-Herb Sauce (page 181)
    or your favorite tomato sauce

2 tablespoons finely chopped fresh basil

½ pound smoked mozzarella cheese,
    cut into ½-inch pieces

¾ cup freshly grated Parmesan cheese

❶ In a deep skillet or a large saucepan, bring the stock to a simmer over medium heat. There should be enough liquid to cover the chicken. Add the chicken and simmer for 12 to 15 minutes, or until just cooked through. Remove from the heat and let the chicken cool in the liquid. Drain and remove the skin. Shred the chicken into bite-sized strips by tearing it into long, thin pieces or slicing it with a knife. Reserve. ❷ Preheat the oven to 425 degrees F. In a large roasting pan, combine the olive oil, leeks, zucchini, and eggplant and stir to coat all the ingredients with the oil. Roast the vegetables, turning them occasionally to keep them from sticking, for 40 to 45 minutes, or until softened. Remove from the oven, let cool, and season with salt and pepper. ❸ Bring a large pot of salted water to a boil. Add the pasta and cook over high heat until nearly al dente, about 12 minutes. Drain well. ❹ Preheat the oven to 400 degrees F. Grease a 9-by-13-inch baking dish. ❺ Transfer the pasta to a large bowl. Pour 3½ cups of the tomato sauce over the pasta and mix well. Add the basil, mozzarella cheese, ¼ cup of the Parmesan cheese, and the reserved chicken and roasted vegetables. Mix well. Taste for seasoning. ❻ Spoon the pasta mixture into the prepared dish and dot the surface with the remaining ½ cup tomato sauce. Sprinkle the remaining ½ cup Parmesan evenly over the top. ❼ Bake the pasta for 20 minutes, or until bubbling hot. Serve immediately.

Advance Preparation: Can be prepared up to 1 day ahead through step 6, covered, and refrigerated. Remove from the refrigerator 30 minutes before baking.

[SERVES 6]

pasta with asparagus and leeks

Fresh asparagus with just a hint of olive oil and a subtle backdrop of sautéed leeks is showcased in this light pasta. Serve as a main course with a hefty sprinkling of Parmesan cheese or use as a bed for stews such as Veal Stew with Tomatoes and Shiitake Mushrooms (page 99).

❶ In a skillet, heat the olive oil over medium heat. Add the leeks and sauté for 5 to 7 minutes, or until softened and golden brown. Add the asparagus and the chicken stock, cover, and steam for 4 to 5 minutes, or until the asparagus is crisp-tender. Add the parsley, salt, and pepper, and set aside. ❷ Meanwhile, bring a large pot of salted water to a boil. Add the pasta and cook over high heat until al dente, about 3 minutes for fresh and 6 for dried. Drain and place in a warmed serving bowl. ❸ Add the vegetables to the pasta and toss to combine. Taste for seasoning. Serve immediately.

[SERVES 4 ➡ 6]

2 tablespoons olive oil

2 leeks, white and light green parts only, cleaned and finely chopped

1 pound asparagus, trimmed and cut into 1 ½-inch lengths

1 cup chicken stock

2 tablespoons finely chopped parsley

salt and freshly ground black pepper

1 pound fresh or dried linguine

angel hair pasta with spring vegetables and red pepper–tomato sauce

Angel hair has become a favorite pasta on the menus of casual restaurants across the country, often paired with a simple tomato-basil sauce. This colorful version is enhanced by a slightly smoky sauce and garden-fresh blanched vegetables. When blanching the vegetables, use a kitchen strainer with a handle to make it easier to lift the vegetables out of the water. This dish also tastes great with the addition of seared scallops.

❶ Fill a saucepan with water and bring to a boil over high heat. Place the asparagus pieces in a kitchen strainer basket with a handle, lower into the boiling water, and cook for 2 to 3 minutes, or until crisp-tender. Immediately transfer the asparagus to a bowl of ice water. Repeat the method to blanch the peas. Drain well. ❷ Bring a large pot of salted water to a boil. Add the pasta and cook for 3 to 4 minutes, or until al dente. ❸ Meanwhile, place the sauce in a saucepan over medium heat and bring to a simmer. Add the asparagus, peas, and yellow pepper and heat just until sauce is hot and the vegetables are warmed through. ❹ Drain the pasta well and place in a serving bowl. Scoop out and reserve ¼ cup of the sauce and add the remaining sauce to the pasta. Toss to coat. Spoon the reserved sauce on top and sprinkle with the parsley and Parmesan cheese. Serve immediately.

[SERVES 4 ➡ 6]

1 pound pencil-thin asparagus, trimmed and cut into 1½-inch lengths

1½ cups frozen petite peas

3 cups Red Pepper–Tomato Sauce (page 182)

1 Peeled Yellow Bell Pepper (page 177), cut into ¼-inch-wide strips

1 pound dried angel hair pasta

1 tablespoon finely chopped parsley

½ cup freshly grated Parmesan cheese

polenta lasagna with tomatoes and peppers

The first polenta lasagna I ever tasted was made with layers of the classic Bolognese and béchamel sauces alternating with the cornmeal filling. This variation takes into account the inherent heaviness of polenta and lightens it up with a fluffy spinach filling and a bold, spicy pepper–tomato sauce. You won't miss the noodles in this crowd pleaser, which is an ideal vegetarian addition to a buffet. Begin with Roasted Eggplant–Garlic Spread (page 23), Parmesan Crisps (page 26), and a glass of California red wine. A double recipe of Mixed Greens with Roasted Beets and Toasted Walnuts (page 51) is a perfect prelude to this satisfying one-dish meal.

1 tablespoon olive oil

1 small onion, very finely chopped

1 garlic clove, minced

½ teaspoon salt

7 cups chicken stock

2 cups instant polenta
    (one 13.2-ounce box)

7 tablespoons freshly grated
    Parmesan cheese

2 packages (10 ounces each) frozen
    chopped spinach, thawed

2 containers (15 ounces each) lowfat
    ricotta cheese

salt and freshly ground black pepper

pinch of freshly grated nutmeg

1 recipe Red Pepper–Tomato Sauce
    (page 182)

2 cups shredded mozzarella cheese
    (about ½ pound)

❶ Lightly spray a 9-by-13-inch baking dish with nonstick cooking spray. In a large saucepan, warm the olive oil over medium heat. Add the onion and sauté for 3 to 5 minutes, or until softened. Add the garlic and sauté for 1 minute more, making sure it does not brown. Add the salt and stock and bring to a rolling boil over medium heat. ❷ In a thin stream (a measuring cup with a lip works well for pouring), very slowly add the polenta, stirring constantly with a wooden spoon. Reduce the heat to low and continue cooking for 3 to 5 minutes, stirring constantly to be sure it doesn't stick, until it is very thick, smooth, and creamy. Stir in 3 tablespoons of the Parmesan cheese. ❸ Pour the polenta into the prepared baking dish, smoothing the top with a rubber spatula if necessary. Let the polenta rest for at least 2 hours to set. ❹ Squeeze out all of the water from the spinach. In a small bowl, mix the spinach with the ricotta cheese. Season with salt, pepper, and nutmeg. ❺ Preheat the oven to 375 degrees F. ❻ Invert the polenta onto a cutting surface. Set the dish aside to use again. Cut the polenta rectangle in half to make 2 rectangles each measuring 9 by 6½ inches. (This will make it easier to transfer the polenta back into the baking dish later on.) Cut a 2-foot long piece of dental floss and hold it taut between your hands. Working with 1 piece of polenta at a time, place the floss against the end farthest from you and pull the floss toward you, through the center of the polenta piece, slicing it in half to give you a top and a bottom layer. (Alternatively, use a serrated knife to slice through the polenta.) Repeat with the second rectangle. ❼ Spoon 1 cup of the Red Pepper–Tomato Sauce evenly on the bottom of the 9-by-13-inch baking dish. Place two of the polenta pieces in the dish to cover the bottom. Spoon half of the spinach-ricotta mixture over the polenta, using the back of a spoon to spread it out, and then sprinkle with 1 cup of the mozzarella and 2 tablespoons of the Parmesan cheese.

Spoon 2 cups of the sauce over the cheese. ❽ Top with the remaining polenta pieces. Spoon the remaining spinach-ricotta mixture evenly over the polenta. Sprinkle the remaining 1 cup mozzarella over the top. Dot with the remaining 1 cup sauce, leaving small gaps between the sauce. Sprinkle with the remaining 2 tablespoons of Parmesan. (The lasagna will be high, slightly above the rim of the dish.) ❾ Place the lasagna dish on a baking sheet to catch any drips. Bake, uncovered, for 30 minutes. Remove from the oven and let sit for 10 minutes. To serve, cut into serving portions and use a spoon or spatula to scoop them out onto individual dishes.

Advance Preparation: The lasagna can be made up to 1 day ahead through step 8, covered, and refrigerated. Remove from the refrigerator 1 hour before baking.

[SERVES 6 ➡ 8]

Pictured on page 105

grilled polenta

This traditional Italian cornmeal porridge has won the hearts of Americans and has been adopted by chefs and home cooks across the nation. While the classic polenta takes about 30 minutes of cooking and stirring, the imported instant (precooked) polenta is ready in a matter of minutes and yields an excellent flavor.

In this basic version, the polenta is grilled, but it can also be served hot and creamy straight from the stove once the cheese and corn have been added. You can stir in all sorts of other flavorings, too, such as fresh goat cheese, roasted peppers, Poblano Chile Pesto (page 61), or Sun-Dried Tomato Pesto (page 180). Overlapping slices of grilled polenta can be topped with Caramelized Fennel and Red Onions (page 185) or used as an accompaniment to Grilled Lime-Cilantro Chicken with Tomatillo Salsa (page 76).

3 tablespoons olive oil

½ onion, very finely chopped

1 garlic clove, minced

½ teaspoon salt

3½ cups chicken stock

1 cup instant polenta
      (half of a 13.2-ounce box)

½ cup corn kernels (about 1 ear of corn)

¼ cup freshly grated Parmesan cheese

❶ Lightly spray an 8-inch square pan with nonstick cooking spray. In a large saucepan, heat 1 tablespoon of the olive oil over medium heat. Add the onion and sauté for 3 to 5 minutes, or until softened. Add the garlic and sauté for 1 minute more, making sure not to brown it. Add the salt and stock, and bring to a rolling boil over medium heat. ❷ In a thin stream (a measuring cup with a lip works well for pouring), very slowly add the polenta, stirring constantly with a wooden spoon. Reduce the heat to low and continue cooking, stirring constantly to be sure it doesn't stick, for 3 to 5 minutes, or until it is very thick, smooth, and creamy. Add the corn and Parmesan and stir to combine until the cheese has melted into the polenta. ❸ Pour the warm polenta into the prepared pan, smoothing the top with a rubber spatula if necessary. Let the polenta rest for 2 hours to set. ❹ Invert the polenta onto a cutting board and cut it into squares or triangles. ❺ Prepare a charcoal or gas grill for medium-high-heat grilling about 3 inches from the fire or place a grill pan on medium-high heat. Oil the grill pan lightly. ❻ Brush both sides of the polenta pieces with the remaining 2 tablespoons oil, and grill for 5 to 7 minutes on each side, or until brown and crispy. Serve immediately.

Advance Preparation: Can be prepared up to 1 day ahead through step 3, covered and refrigerated. Bring to room temperature before continuing.

[SERVES 4 ➡ 6]

herbed vegetable rice

Consider this versatile rice when you need a side dish to serve with seafood, chicken, or meats. A jazzed-up version of basic white rice, it is my standby when I am looking for an accompaniment that will add color and texture, yet won't overpower whatever else I am serving.

❶ Heat a small skillet over medium-low heat. Add the almonds and toast, tossing often, for 2 to 3 minutes, or until lightly browned. Remove to a plate and reserve. ❷ In a saucepan over high heat, bring the stock to a boil. Add the rice, salt, and pepper and stir with a fork. Cover tightly, reduce the heat to low, and simmer for 20 minutes, or until tender. ❸ Meanwhile, in a skillet, heat the olive oil over medium heat. Add the leek and sauté for 3 to 5 minutes, or until softened. Add the bell pepper and zucchini and sauté for about 5 minutes, or until the vegetables are cooked but still slightly crisp. ❹ When the rice is ready, add the sautéed vegetables, toasted almonds, and parsley. Stir and toss gently with a fork. Taste for seasoning. Transfer the rice to a serving bowl and serve immediately.

Advance Preparation: Can be prepared up to 2 hours ahead, covered, and kept at room temperature. Reheat carefully in the top of a double boiler over medium heat.

[SERVES 4 ➡ 6]

3 tablespoons almonds

2 cups chicken stock

1 cup long-grain white rice

salt and freshly ground black pepper

2 tablespoons olive oil

1 small leek, white and light green parts
*   only, cleaned and finely chopped*

½ red bell pepper, seeded and cut into
*   ½-inch dice*

1 zucchini, cut into ½-inch dice

2 tablespoons finely chopped parsley

garden vegetable stew with couscous

Exciting vegetarian main courses are finding their way onto American bistro menus from coast to coast. This dish is based on the traditional Moroccan idea of a stew served over couscous, but here a simpler blend of spices, fresh herbs, and golden raisins accents the mélange of squash and other vegetables. Since the couscous quickly absorbs liquid, be sure the stew has plenty of stock, wine, and juices from the vegetables. Feel free to add more liquid as needed. For a variation, add canned garbanzo beans to the stew to make it even heartier.

❶ In a large saucepan or Dutch oven, heat 1 tablespoon of the olive oil over medium heat. Add the onions and sauté for 3 to 5 minutes, or until softened. Add the winter squash, salt, and pepper, and cook, stirring often, for about 15 minutes, or until the squash begins to brown slightly. Stir in the thyme, pour in the stock and wine, and simmer, stirring occasionally, for about 10 minutes more, or until the squash is just tender. ❷ Meanwhile, heat the remaining 1 tablespoon olive oil in a large skillet over medium heat. Add the zucchini, yellow squashes, and mushrooms and sauté for about 5 minutes, or just until softened. Add the garlic and tomatoes and sauté for 1 minute longer. ❸ When the winter squash is just tender, add the zucchini mixture and stir to combine. Let the stew simmer for about 5 minutes, adding more wine or stock if the stew seems too dry. Stir in the vinegar, 3 tablespoons of the parsley, and the basil, and taste for seasoning. ❹ Meanwhile, bring the stock to a boil in a saucepan. Add the butter, salt, and pepper, and stir in the couscous. Cover the pan tightly, remove from the heat, and let stand for 5 minutes. Uncover and fluff the couscous with a fork. Add the raisins and 1 tablespoon of the parsley and stir to combine. ❺ To serve, spoon the warm couscous into a serving bowl or individual shallow bowls. Top with warm vegetable stew, garnish with the remaining 1 tablespoon parsley, and serve immediately.

Advance Preparation: Can be prepared up to 4 hours ahead through step 3, covered, and kept at room temperature. Reheat gently when ready to serve. The vegetables will absorb some of the liquid, so you may need to add extra stock.

[SERVES 4 ➡ 6]

2 tablespoons olive oil

1 large onion, finely chopped

1 butternut or acorn squash, 1 ½ to
    2 pounds, halved, seeded, peeled,
    and cut into 1-inch cubes

salt and freshly ground black pepper

1 teaspoon finely chopped fresh thyme

1 cup chicken stock

½ cup dry white wine

3 zucchini, cut into ½-inch cubes

3 yellow summer squashes, cut into
    ½-inch cubes

1 pound mushrooms, cut into
    ½-inch wedges

2 garlic cloves, minced

3 tomatoes, peeled, seeded, and diced

2 tablespoons balsamic vinegar

5 tablespoons finely chopped parsley

2 tablespoons finely chopped fresh basil

3 cups chicken stock, water, or a
    combination

1 tablespoon unsalted butter

salt and freshly ground black pepper

2 cups quick-cooking couscous

½ cup golden raisins, soaked in boiling
    water to cover for 5 minutes
    and drained

wild rice pilaf with dried fruit and toasted pine nuts

Wild rice is actually not a rice at all, but the seed of an aquatic grass. This gourmet grain, with its nutty flavor and chewy texture, goes especially well with poultry or game. Adding long-grain white rice, toasted nuts and dried fruits reduces the richness of the wild rice, as well as the expense. Serve the pilaf with Crispy Roasted Duck with Black Currant–Plum Sauce (page 86).

¼ cup pine nuts

1 teaspoon olive oil

3 scallions, white and light green parts
    only, finely chopped

3 cups water

¾ cup wild rice

¾ cup long-grain white rice

2 tablespoons golden raisins

2 tablespoons dried cranberries

salt and freshly ground black pepper

1 tablespoon finely chopped parsley

❶ Heat a small skillet over medium-low heat. Add the pine nuts and toast, tossing often, for 2 to 3 minutes, or until they are lightly browned. Remove to a plate and reserve. ❷ In the same skillet, heat the olive oil over medium-low heat. Add the scallions and sauté for 1 to 2 minutes, or until softened. Set aside. ❸ Pour 1½ cups water into each of 2 small saucepans. Place them over high heat and bring to a boil. ❹ To one saucepan, add the wild rice, cover tightly, reduce the heat to low and simmer for 30 minutes. After 30 minutes, remove from the heat and let sit, covered, for 10 minutes. ❺ To the other saucepan, add the white rice, cover tightly, reduce the heat to low, and simmer for 15 to 20 minutes, or until the liquid is absorbed. Remove from the heat and let sit, covered, for 5 minutes. ❻ To serve, transfer the wild rice and the white rice to a serving bowl, add the sautéed scallions, toasted pine nuts, raisins, dried cranberries, salt, pepper, and parsley. Stir and toss gently with a fork. Taste for seasoning. Serve immediately.

Advance Preparation: Can be prepared up to 4 hours ahead through step 2 and kept at room temperature.

[SERVES 4 ➡ 6]

white bean stew with toasted bread crumbs

White beans become creamy as they cook, allowing the juices to thicken slightly. A good shot of balsamic vinegar heightens the flavor of the beans in this simple stew. Keep in mind that there are variables when cooking with beans. For example, older legumes may take longer to break down and become creamy.

These Tuscan-style beans are also delicious served right out of the pot if you don't have time to finish them in the oven with the bread crumbs. Serve them as an accompaniment to Braised Lamb Shanks with Merlot and Prunes (page 100). They are also an excellent side dish to Grilled Veal Chops with Fresh Thyme (page 97) or Grilled Entrecôte (page 93). This stew is a wonderful main-course luncheon dish as well, preceded by an interesting mix of fresh greens. If you are serving this as a main course or first course, present it in shallow soup bowls and grate the Parmesan at the table.

❶ Soak the beans overnight in cold water to cover generously. Or use a quick-soak method: Bring the beans to a boil in water just to cover, boil for 2 minutes, remove from the heat, cover, and let stand for 1 hour. Drain the beans and set aside. ❷ In a Dutch oven or similar pot, heat the olive oil over medium heat. Add the onion and sauté for 3 to 5 minutes, or until soft. Add the garlic and sauté for another minute. Add the ¼ cup balsamic vinegar, stock, and beans. Bring to a boil, reduce the heat to low, cover, and simmer for about 2¼ hours, or until the beans are tender and falling apart, pushing down some of the beans with the back of a spoon to create a creamy consistency. Uncover and reduce for 5 to 10 minutes, or until slightly thickened. ❸ Add the spinach, recover, and braise, for 3 more minutes or until slightly wilted, stirring once. Add the salt, pepper, and the remaining 1 tablespoon balsamic vinegar, and mix to combine. Taste for seasoning. ❹ To serve, preheat the broiler. Spoon the beans into an oven-proof gratin dish. In a small bowl, stir together the Parmesan, bread crumbs, and parsley, and sprinkle evenly over the beans. Place under the broiler for 3 to 4 minutes, or until the bread crumbs and cheese are nicely browned. Serve immediately.

Advance Preparation: Can be prepared up to 1 day ahead through step 3, covered, and refrigerated. Bring to room temperature, place in a baking dish, and reheat for 20 minutes in an oven at 350 degrees F before broiling.

[SERVES 6]

2 cups dried white beans such as Great
    Northern, rinsed and picked over
2 tablespoons olive oil
1 onion, finely chopped
2 garlic cloves, minced
¼ cup plus 1 tablespoon balsamic vinegar
5 cups chicken stock
1 large bunch spinach, cleaned, stemmed,
    and coarsely shredded
salt and freshly ground black pepper
¼ cup freshly grated Parmesan cheese
¼ cup toasted bread crumbs
1 tablespoon finely chopped parsley

spicy black beans with island salsa

These long-simmered black beans combine spicy Latin seasonings with the cool sweetness of the tropics. What makes this dish so spectacular is the resulting contrast of textures and flavors. The flavor actually improves if the dish is refrigerated overnight after cooking, so plan accordingly. If you're a vegetarian, eliminate the ham hock and add a chipotle chile instead. Serve the beans with warm tortillas and your favorite grilled sausage, and top the whole dish with Island Salsa.

2 cups dried black beans, rinsed and
    picked over

2 onions, halved

2 red bell peppers, halved and seeded

1 jalapeño chile, seeded and coarsely
    chopped

1 teaspoon finely chopped fresh oregano
    or ½ teaspoon dried

1 teaspoon ground cumin

1 large ham hock, about 1 pound

3 garlic cloves, peeled but left whole

2 teaspoons salt

2 tablespoons vegetable oil

1 large onion, finely chopped

1 large red bell pepper, seeded and finely
    chopped

2 garlic cloves, minced

¼ cup balsamic vinegar

¼ teaspoon cayenne pepper

salt

1 cup Island Salsa (page 184)

❶ Soak the beans overnight in cold water to cover generously. Or use a quick-soak method: Bring the beans to a boil in water just to cover, boil for 2 minutes, remove from the heat, cover, and let stand for 1 hour. ❷ Drain the beans and put them in a Dutch oven. Add water to cover generously (about 2 quarts). Add the halved onions, halved bell peppers, jalapeño, oregano, cumin, ham hock, garlic, and salt. Bring to a boil, reduce the heat to low and simmer, uncovered, for 1½ hours, or until the mixture is slightly thickened and the beans are cooked. ❸ Remove all the large vegetable pieces and the ham hock and discard. Drain the beans, reserving ½ cup of the bean liquid. Return the beans to the Dutch oven. ❹ In a skillet, heat the vegetable oil over medium-high heat. Add the chopped onions and sauté for about 3 minutes, or until slightly softened. Add the chopped bell pepper and sauté for 3 minutes longer. Add the minced garlic and sauté for another minute. ❺ Place the onion mixture in a food processor fitted with the metal blade and purée. Add the purée to the beans, along with the balsamic vinegar, cayenne pepper, and salt. Stir to combine and taste for seasoning. Add the reserved bean liquid if the beans are too dry. Cover and refrigerate overnight. ❻ To serve, remove the beans from the refrigerator and bring to room temperature for 1 hour. Preheat the oven to 350 degrees F. Place the beans in the oven for 30 minutes. Serve with the salsa on the side.

Advance Preparation: Can be prepared up to 3 days ahead, covered, and refrigerated. Remove the beans from the refrigerator 1 hour before reheating. The salsa can be prepared up to 1 day ahead, covered, and refrigerated.

[SERVES 6]

Vegetables and Potatoes

roasted summer tomatoes

The first time I ever tasted these tomatoes was at a restaurant called Tetou in a little town in the south of France named Juan-les-Pins. The meal is still vivid in my mind: almost-burnt, caramelized tomatoes with a touch of thyme presented in a pottery gratin dish. This was a taste memory I had to re-create. I have found that using a ceramic gratin dish like the kind made by Le Creuset results in the most evenly caramelized tomatoes. Another thing to remember is that tomatoes vary widely in the amount of juice they exude, so just add a bit of water if you find the pan is dry during roasting.

6 large tomatoes, halved

1 teaspoon sugar

2 tablespoons olive oil

salt and freshly ground black pepper

Topping

¼ cup coarse fresh French bread crumbs

2 tablespoons finely chopped parsley

1 teaspoon finely chopped fresh thyme

2 tablespoons olive oil

❶ Preheat the oven to 325 degrees F. Oil a 9-by-13-inch ceramic baking dish. Arrange the tomatoes cut-sides up so they fit snugly in the dish. Sprinkle the sugar evenly over the tomatoes. Drizzle the olive oil over the tomatoes and season with salt and pepper. ❷ Roast for 1½ to 1¾ hours, or until browned and slightly shriveled. Halfway through, poke the tomatoes with a fork to help release some of the juices. Spoon the juices over the tomatoes a few times as they cook. ❸ When the tomatoes are cooked, remove the excess juices from the dish with a bulb baster and place in a small saucepan. Place over medium heat for about 5 minutes, or until reduced and slightly thickened. Remove from the heat and reserve. ❹ Prepare the topping: Combine all the topping ingredients except the oil, and taste for seasoning. Sprinkle the mixture over the cooked tomatoes, then drizzle the olive oil on top, along with the reduced juices. ❺ Roast for another 20 to 30 minutes, or until the tomatoes are crusty golden brown. Serve hot or at room temperature.

Advance Preparation: Can be prepared up to 8 hours ahead and kept at room temperature. Serve at room temperature or reheat in an oven at 325 degrees F for about 15 minutes.

[SERVES 6]

roasted seasonal vegetables

Carrots, baby new potatoes, zucchini, and leeks are just a sampling of the array of vegetables you can use in this basic recipe. During the fall months, add squashes, yellow or red onions, and mushrooms. In the summer, use tomatoes, bell peppers, and fresh-picked corn.

High-heat roasting produces a crisp outer skin and moist inner flesh. Vegetables that have an abundance of natural sugars, like carrots and onions, become especially delicious, since the sugars caramelize and enhance their flavors. Be sure to use a large roasting pan to give the vegetables plenty of room for even roasting, and stir often to brown the vegetables uniformly and prevent sticking. Cooking times may vary slightly, depending on the type of vegetable, its freshness, and its thickness, so taste a few of the larger pieces to make sure they're done.

❶ Preheat the oven to 400 degrees F. In a large roasting pan, combine the eggplant, carrots, zucchini, leek, potatoes and garlic cloves and toss to combine. Drizzle with 2 tablespoons of the olive oil. Add the thyme, salt, and pepper, and mix well, being sure to coat all the vegetables evenly.
❷ Roast for 30 minutes. Using long oven mitts to protect your hands, turn the vegetables every 10 minutes as they roast. Then, add the remaining 1 tablespoon oil and continue roasting for 30 more minutes, turning once more at the midway point. The mixture should be brown and caramelized.
❸ Taste for seasoning. Spoon the vegetables into a large serving bowl and garnish with the parsley. Serve immediately.

Advance Preparation: Can be prepared up to 4 hours ahead, kept at room temperature, and reheated in an oven at 350 degrees F for about 20 minutes.

[SERVES 4 ➡ 6]

1 large eggplant, unpeeled, cut into
*   1-inch chunks*
3 carrots, peeled and cut into
*   1-inch chunks*
2 zucchini, cut into 1-inch chunks
1 leek, white and light green parts only,
*   cleaned and sliced*
1 pound baby new potatoes, quartered
5 garlic cloves, peeled but left whole
3 tablespoons olive oil
1 teaspoon finely chopped fresh thyme
salt and freshly ground black pepper
2 tablespoons finely chopped parsley,
*   for garnish*

oven-roasted ratatouille

This classic Mediterranean vegetable mélange is roasted rather than sautéed to reduce the amount of oil. The ratatouille can be served as a side dish, or as a bed for Baked Eggs with Oven-Roasted Ratatouille (page 168). As an option, mix in 2 tablespoons Basic Pesto (page 179) right at the end.

1 eggplant, unpeeled, cut into 1-inch cubes

1 large onion, sliced

1 red bell pepper, seeded and cut into 1-inch squares

2 tablespoons olive oil

2 teaspoons finely chopped fresh thyme

salt and freshly ground black pepper

¼ pound mushrooms, quartered

1 garlic clove, minced

3 large tomatoes, peeled, seeded, and diced

2 yellow summer squashes, cut into ½-inch chunks

2 zucchini, cut into ½-inch chunks

3 tablespoons finely chopped parsley

2 tablespoons finely chopped fresh basil, for garnish

❶ Preheat the oven to 425 degrees F. In a large roasting pan, combine the eggplant, onion and bell pepper. Drizzle with the olive oil and toss to coat the vegetables. Sprinkle with the thyme, salt, and pepper, and toss again. Roast, uncovered, for 20 to 25 minutes or until vegetables begin to soften. Using long oven mitts to protect your hands, stir the vegetables twice as they roast. ❷ Add the mushrooms, garlic, and tomatoes, and toss to mix well. Return the vegetables to the oven and roast for 10 to 15 minutes, stirring once. ❸ Add the summer squashes, zucchini, and 2 tablespoons of the parsley, and toss to mix well. Return to the oven and roast for 30 to 35 minutes, or until all the squashes are tender. ❹ To serve, transfer the vegetable mixture to a serving dish, using a slotted spoon to drain off the excess liquid. Discard the liquid. Sprinkle the vegetables with the remaining 1 tablespoon parsley and the basil, and mix to combine. Taste for seasoning. Serve hot, at room temperature, or cold.

Advance Preparation: Can be prepared up to 2 days ahead, covered, and refrigerated. Gently reheat on the stove or in the oven before serving, or serve at room temperature or cold.

[SERVES 6]

braised spinach

Large bunches of spinach exposed to heat wilt down quickly to remarkably smaller servings. This comforting dish uses just enough butter and oil to balance any bitterness in the spinach, and sautéed garlic and shallots give the dish a Mediterranean accent. This can be easily doubled using a very large Dutch oven. Serve this simple, versatile dish with Grilled Veal Chops with Fresh Thyme (page 97) or Whole Roasted Striped Bass on Sliced Potatoes (page 60).

❶ Wash the spinach well in several changes of cold water to remove all of the sand and mud. Discard any heavy stems or yellow leaves and shake off excess water. ❷ In a large Dutch oven, melt the butter with the olive oil over medium heat. Add the shallots and sauté for 2 to 3 minutes, or until soft. Add the garlic, salt, and pepper, and sauté for another minute. ❸ Add all of the spinach, pushing it down to make it fit in the pan and turning it with tongs to coat it with the shallot-garlic mixture. Cover tightly and steam for 2 to 3 minutes, turning the spinach with tongs after the first minute. ❹ Uncover the pan and continue to cook, turning with tongs, for about 1 minute or until the spinach is wilted. You'll find that there will be excess liquid from the spinach in the bottom of the pan, so use tongs to transfer the spinach to serving plates. Serve immediately.

[SERVES 4]

3 bunches spinach

2 tablespoons unsalted butter

2 tablespoons olive oil

2 shallots, finely chopped

2 garlic cloves, minced

salt and freshly ground black pepper

garden vegetable sauté

In this colorful vegetable medley, matchstick-cut vegetables are quickly blanched in boiling water to cook them slightly. Then the vegetables are sautéed in a little butter and oil to accentuate their flavor. The end result is a wonderful side dish of delicate, crisp vegetables that is perfect alongside almost any main course dish.

❶ Fill a large saucepan with lightly salted water and bring to a boil. Place the carrots in a kitchen strainer basket with a handle, and immerse in the boiling water for 1 minute. Drain and set aside. Place the celery, yellow squash, and zucchini in the strainer basket and immerse in the boiling water for 30 seconds. Drain and set aside. Place the green beans in the strainer basket and immerse in the boiling water for 2 minutes. Drain and set aside. ❷ In a skillet, heat the butter and oil over medium heat. Add the onion and sauté for 5 to 7 minutes, or until softened and slightly browned. Add the carrots, celery, yellow squash, zucchini, and beans and continue sautéing for another 3 minutes, or until cooked through but not soft. Add the salt, pepper, and parsley and mix well. ❸ Taste for seasoning. Transfer to a serving bowl and serve immediately.

Advance Preparation: The vegetables can be blanched up to 1 day ahead (step 1), wrapped in plastic wrap, and refrigerated. Bring to room temperature before sautéing.

[SERVES 4 ➡ 6]

4 carrots, peeled and cut into matchsticks

3 stalks celery, peeled and cut into matchsticks

1 yellow squash, cut into matchsticks

1 zucchini, cut into matchsticks

¼ pound slender green beans, trimmed

1 tablespoon unsalted butter

1 tablespoon olive oil

¼ red onion, thinly sliced

salt and freshly ground black pepper

1 tablespoon finely chopped parsley

butternut squash and carrot purée with ginger

Naturally sweet butternut squash and carrots make a wonderful cold-weather purée. Fresh ginger and a hint of maple syrup finish off this beautiful orange side dish. Spoon or pipe the purée onto plates with Roasted Cornish Hens with Orange-Honey-Mustard Glaze (page 81) or Crispy Roasted Duck with Black Currant–Plum Sauce (page 86).

*2 butternut squashes, about 3 pounds
    total, peeled, seeded, and cut into
    1-inch cubes*

6 carrots, peeled and cut into 1-inch cubes

1 teaspoon ground ginger

2 teaspoons maple syrup

3 tablespoons unsalted butter

2 tablespoons olive oil

salt and white pepper

*1 tablespoon finely chopped parsley,
    for garnish*

❶ Steam the squashes and carrots in a steamer basket over boiling water for 15 to 20 minutes, or until tender. ❷ In a food processor fitted with the metal blade, combine the steamed vegetables, ginger, maple syrup, butter, olive oil, salt, and pepper. Process until puréed, scraping down the sides of the work bowl as needed. Taste for seasoning. ❸ To serve, transfer the purée to a serving bowl, or spoon into a pastry bag and pipe large rosettes onto individual plates. Sprinkle with the parsley and serve immediately.

Advance Preparation: Can be prepared up to 1 day ahead, covered, and refrigerated. Gently reheat in a saucepan just before serving.

[SERVES 6]

root vegetable purée

Root vegetables fill the stalls of outdoor markets during the colder months, just calling out for creative uses to brighten gray days. This flavorful trio of vegetables seems to bring out the best in each, and an added bonus is that it's quick to prepare. For a more formal presentation, use a pastry bag and pipe the purée right onto the plate.

❶ Fill a large saucepan with water, add the turnips, parsnips, and rutabagas, and place over medium-high heat. Bring to a boil, cover loosely, and boil until the vegetables are tender, 15 to 17 minutes. Drain well. ❷ In a food processor fitted with the metal blade, combine the turnips, parsnips, rutabagas, and garlic, and process until smooth. Add the olive oil, butter, nutmeg, sour cream, buttermilk, salt and pepper and process to mix well, stopping to scrape down the sides of the work bowl as necessary. Taste for seasoning. ❸ To serve, transfer the purée to a serving bowl, or spoon into a pastry bag and pipe large rosettes onto individual plates. Sprinkle with the parsley and serve immediately.

Advance Preparation: Can be prepared up to 1 day ahead, covered, and refrigerated. Gently reheat in a saucepan just before serving.

[SERVES 6]

*1 pound turnips, peeled and cut into
    1-inch cubes*

*1 pound parsnips, peeled and cut into
    1-inch cubes*

*1 pound rutabagas, peeled and cut into
    1-inch cubes*

2 garlic cloves, minced

2 tablespoons olive oil

1 tablespoon unsalted butter

¼ teaspoon freshly grated nutmeg

1 tablespoon sour cream

3 tablespoons buttermilk

salt and white pepper

*1 tablespoon finely chopped parsley,
    for garnish*

spinach-carrot terrine
with red pepper-tomato sauce

This colorful terrine makes an impressive first course, side dish, or vegetarian main course. Spinach leaves run through the center of a light carrot-and-shiitake cheese custard. Spoon Red Pepper–Tomato Sauce over the terrine and serve chilled, warm, or at room temperature.

2½ pounds carrots, peeled and sliced
    ¼-inch thick

3 tablespoons olive oil

½ pound fresh shiitake mushrooms, sliced

2 bunches spinach, cleaned, stemmed,
    and dried

4 large eggs, lightly beaten

½ cup milk

2 cups shredded Gruyère cheese (about
    ½ pound)

salt and freshly ground black pepper

pinch of freshly grated nutmeg

1 cup Red Pepper–Tomato Sauce, heated
    (page 182)

❶ Steam the carrots in a steamer basket over boiling water for 5 to 7 minutes, or until crisp-tender. In a food processor fitted with the metal blade, chop the carrots into small dice using the on-off pulse. Remove to a bowl. ❷ In a skillet, heat 2 tablespoons of the olive oil over medium heat. Add the mushrooms and sauté for 3 minutes, or until softened. Using a slotted spoon, remove the mushrooms to paper towels to drain well. In a food processor fitted with the metal blade, chop the mushrooms into small dice using the on-off pulse. Add to the carrots. ❸ In a large skillet, heat the remaining olive oil over medium-high heat. Add the spinach and sauté for about 3 minutes, or until softened but still bright green (you may have to do this in batches). Place the spinach in a strainer and squeeze out all the liquid by pushing down on the spinach with the back of a spoon. In the food processor fitted with the metal blade, coarsely chop the spinach using the on-off pulse. Set aside. ❹ Preheat the oven to 400 degrees F. ❺ Generously butter a 9-by-5-by-2½-inch loaf pan. In a bowl, wisk together the eggs, milk, and cheese. Add the carrots and mushrooms and combine thoroughly. Add the salt, pepper, and nutmeg. Pour half of the mixture into the prepared loaf pan. Spread the spinach evenly over the top and then pour in the remaining carrot mixture, smoothing the surface with a rubber spatula if necessary. ❻ Place the loaf pan in a larger baking pan and place in the oven. Carefully pour almost-boiling water into the larger pan to come halfway up the sides of the loaf pan. Bake for 45 minutes, or until the top is browned and the filling is set. Remove from the oven and let rest for 15 minutes. ❼ To serve, invert onto a platter, then turn upright. Pour the sauce around the terrine and serve warm. Or slice the terrine and serve on individual plates surrounded by the sauce.

Advance Preparation: The sauce can be prepared up to 3 days ahead, covered, and refrigerated. The terrine can be prepared up to 2 days ahead, covered, and refrigerated. Serve the terrine chilled or at room temperature, or reheat in an oven at 350 degrees F for 20 minutes.

[SERVES 6 ➡ 8]

potato-vegetable gratin

Relying on vegetables, fresh herbs, and cheese, this gratin is full of flavor without the need for cream, and it can be made year-round. Just substitute canned diced and drained tomatoes if fresh tomatoes are not at their prime. Look for the organic canned variety that have extra flavor and a deep red color. Try this with Grilled Entrecôte (page 93) or Lemon-Rosemary Roasted Chicken (page 74).

3 tablespoons olive oil

*1 leek, white and light green parts only,
    cleaned and finely chopped*

*1 yellow bell pepper, seeded and thinly
    sliced*

3 zucchini, thinly sliced

*4 tomatoes, peeled, seeded, and coarsely
    chopped, or 2 cups drained canned
    diced tomatoes*

*1 teaspoon Roasted Garlic Purée (page 175)
    or 2 garlic cloves, minced*

salt and freshly ground black pepper

1 teaspoon finely chopped fresh thyme

¼ cup finely chopped fresh basil

*3 baking or Yukon Gold potatoes, peeled
    and cut into ¼-inch-thick slices*

1 cup shredded Gruyère cheese

❶ Preheat the oven to 400 degrees F. Spray a deep, 3-quart baking dish with nonstick cooking spray. ❷ In a large skillet, heat the olive oil over medium heat. Add the leek and sauté for 3 to 5 minutes, or until soft. Add the bell pepper and zucchini and sauté for 3 to 5 minutes, or until softened. Add the tomatoes and sauté for 3 to 5 minutes until the excess liquid evaporates. Add the garlic, salt, pepper, thyme, and 2 tablespoons of the basil and mix well. Remove from the heat. ❸ Place half of the potatoes in the dish, overlapping the slices. Spread half of the vegetable mixture over the potato slices. Sprinkle ½ cup of the Gruyère evenly over the vegetables. Repeat the layers, ending with the cheese. Cover tightly with aluminum foil. ❹ Bake for 45 minutes. Remove the foil and bake for 30 to 35 minutes longer, or until the potatoes are tender and the top is browned. Serve warm garnished with the remaining 2 tablespoons basil.

Advance Preparation: Can be prepared up to 1 day ahead, covered, and refrigerated. Bring to room temperature, cover with foil, and reheat in an oven at 350 degrees F for 20 to 30 minutes.

[SERVES 6 ➡ 8]

roasted new potatoes with leeks

These tasty nuggets go well with most any grilled or roasted dish. If you want to experiment with other potatoes, try Yukon Gold or small purple potatoes. Each one adds its own character to this simple dish. The potatoes pair well with Broiled Snapper with Poblano Chile Pesto (page 61) or Roasted Cornish Hens with Orange-Honey-Mustard Glaze (page 81).

❶ Preheat the oven to 425 degrees F. ❷ Bring a large pot of water to a boil, add the potatoes, and boil for 5 minutes. Drain the potatoes and pat dry with paper towels. ❸ In a roasting pan, combine the potatoes, olive oil, salt, and pepper. Use a large spoon to coat the potatoes evenly with the oil. ❹ Roast for 20 minutes, stirring after 10 minutes. Sprinkle the potatoes evenly with the leeks, and continue roasting for 20 minutes longer, stirring the potatoes after 10 minutes, until they are brown and crispy and the leeks are golden. Taste for seasoning. ❺ To serve, transfer the potatoes to a serving bowl and garnish with the parsley.

Advance Preparation: Can be prepared up to 4 hours ahead, kept at room temperature, and reheated in an oven at 350 degrees F for 15 minutes.

[SERVES 4 ➡ 6]

2 pounds small red new potatoes, unpeeled
2 tablespoons olive oil
salt and freshly ground black pepper
1 large leek, white and light green parts
*   only, cleaned and coarsely chopped*
2 tablespoons finely chopped parsley,
*   for garnish*

perfect mashed potatoes

This King of Comfort Food can be prepared using just about any potato: Yellow Finn, Yukon Gold, Red Bliss, or russets, to name just a few. Keep in mind you will have a fluffier mashed potato if you use russet potatoes, and a creamier consistency if you use red, yellow, or white potatoes. Leave the peels on if you want to increase the vitamin content of the dish and you don't mind the look and texture of the peels. For different flavorings, add Sun-Dried Tomato Pesto (page 180), freshly grated Parmesan cheese, horseradish cream, Roasted Garlic Purée (page 175), or caramelized fennel. For low-fat versions, replace the butter and half-and-half with warmed chicken stock or skim milk.

*3 pounds potatoes (see recipe introduction),
    peeled and cut into 3-inch pieces*
1 teaspoon salt
3 tablespoons unsalted butter
1 cup half-and-half
salt and white pepper

❶ Place the potatoes in a large bowl of cold water to cover for 5 minutes to remove excess starch, then drain. ❷ Bring a large pot of water to a boil over high heat and add the salt and potatoes. Boil for 15 to 20 minutes, or until the potatoes are fork tender. ❸ Meanwhile, heat the butter and half-and-half together in a saucepan over medium heat until small bubbles appear on the surface. ❹ Drain the potatoes well in a colander and return to the pot. Dry the potatoes over high heat for 1 to 2 minutes, tossing them until all the moisture has evaporated. ❺ Immediately pass the potatoes through a potato ricer into a large bowl, or mash them with a potato masher in a large bowl if the peels have been left on. Add the heated butter and half-and-half mixture to the potatoes and whip them with a wooden spoon or wire whisk to a smooth but not soupy consistency. ❻ When the liquid is absorbed, add the salt and pepper (along with any flavorings mentioned in the recipe introduction, if desired) and taste for seasoning. Transfer to a serving bowl and serve immediately.

Advance Preparation: Can be prepared up to 2 hours ahead, covered, and kept at room temperature. Reheat gently in the top of a double boiler over medium heat. Add extra half-and-half as needed for the correct consistency. Adjust the seasonings.

[SERVES 6]

crispy potato pancakes

Not only are these a snap to make in great quantity, but they freeze beautifully. This one-step food-processor method makes the usually tedious work of assembling the pancakes doable for even the busiest cook. No need to shred the potatoes; the metal blade in the food processor does a great job with near-perfect results.

Remember, you can make as many batches of potato pancake batter as you want, pour it into a large bowl, and fry the pancakes as needed. I like to use a small ice cream scoop to drop them into the hot oil. You can also use a ladle or large tablespoon. Serve them on their own with a hefty dollop of Cinnamon Spice Applesauce (page 186) or with Braised Brisket of Beef with Onions and Garlic (page 92). These pancakes also are excellent as a first course topped with your favorite caviar or smoked salmon. For a Southwest touch, crown with a dollop of spicy salsa and sour cream.

❶ Combine the onion and eggs in a food processor fitted with the metal blade and purée until smooth and fluffy. Add the potatoes and pulse until the mixture is finely chopped but still retains some texture. Add the salt, pepper and flour and process quickly to combine. Do not overprocess. Pour the batter into a bowl. ❷ Cover the batter with plastic wrap (to prevent discoloration) and let sit for 15 minutes. ❸ Pour oil to a depth of ¾ inch into a large nonstick skillet. Place over medium-high heat. Pour 1 tablespoon of the batter into the skillet to test the oil. If it is hot enough, the pancake will begin to sizzle and brown. Spoon tablespoons of the batter into the skillet, making sure that there's a little room around each spoonful. Flatten them with the back of a spoon and use the spatula to round out the sides, if necessary. Fry the pancakes for about 3 minutes, or until they are golden brown on the first side. Turn them and fry until brown on the second side, about 2 minutes. ❹ Using a slotted spatula, transfer the pancakes to a baking sheet lined with 2 layers of paper towels and let drain briefly. Arrange on a platter and serve with the applesauce.

Advance Preparation: To freeze the potato pancakes, let drain on the paper towels, then place them on a double sheet of aluminum foil and enclose them tightly in the foil. Make sure the pancakes are completely cool and then place on a flat surface in the freezer. When ready to serve, preheat the oven to 425 degrees F and place the foil packets on a baking sheet. Remove the top sheet of foil so that the pancakes will bake evenly. Bake the frozen pancakes for 5 to 7 minutes or until they are brown and crispy.

1 onion, quartered

2 large eggs

*2 baking potatoes, about 1 pound, peeled
    and cut into 1-inch cubes*

salt and freshly ground black pepper

2 tablespoons all-purpose flour

vegetable oil, for frying

*1 cup Cinnamon Spice Applesauce
    (page 186), for serving*

MAKES 12-14 PANCAKES [SERVES 4 ➡ 6]

shoestring potatoes

A mandoline, or French vegetable slicer, is a handy kitchen tool, especially for cutting perfect shoestrings. Settings can be adjusted to accommodate different vegetables and a variety of slices, including chips and waffles. If you don't have a deep-fat fryer, use a deep, heavy saucepan with a metal frying basket with a handle. For a spicy variation, season the warm potatoes with a combination of paprika, cayenne, salt, and black pepper. I also like to make an herb-and-cheese version by tossing the warm potatoes with Parmesan cheese and parsley. These potatoes go well with Grilled Entrecôte (page 93), or Grilled Veal Sausages with Sautéed Apples and Caramelized Fennel and Red Onions (page 98). They are also great with Goat Cheese–Stuffed Hamburgers with Two-Olive Spread (page 94).

2 pounds baking potatoes
vegetable oil, for deep-frying
salt

❶ Peel the potatoes and cut lengthwise into slices ¼ inch thick. Then cut each slice lengthwise into strips ¼ inch wide. Place in a large bowl of water to cover for 5 minutes to remove excess starch, then drain. ❷ Pour oil to a depth of 2 inches into a deep-fat fryer or deep, heavy saucepan. Heat the oil to 375 degrees F. While the oil is heating, thoroughly dry the potatoes with kitchen towels (so the water won't spatter when it hits the oil), and place a small batch in the frying basket. ❸ Fry the potatoes, stirring with long tongs to prevent them from sticking together, for 8 to 10 minutes, or until golden brown and crisp. ❹ Lift the basket, draining as much oil as possible, then spread the fries on a baking sheet lined with paper towels to soak up the excess oil. Add the salt, taste for seasoning, and serve immediately.

[SERVES 4]

Desserts

roasted pears in red wine–caramel sauce

Bosc pears are my first choice for this classic bistro dessert because they have an aromatic spiciness and creamy texture that holds up well during cooking. With their long tapered necks and russet skin, these pears look like works of art when they come out of the oven glazed in the red wine–caramel sauce. Serve them alone, with biscotti, or alongside vanilla ice cream.

3 cups red wine (about 1 bottle)

1 cup sugar

1 cinnamon stick

finely chopped zest of 1 lemon

1 vanilla bean, slit open

8 ripe Bosc pears, with stems attached

fresh mint leaves, for garnish

8 biscotti (optional)

1 quart vanilla ice cream (optional)

❶ Preheat the oven to 350 degrees F. Combine the red wine, sugar, cinnamon stick, lemon zest, and vanilla bean in a saucepan and bring to a simmer over medium heat, stirring to dissolve the sugar. Remove and discard the cinnamon stick. ❷ Core each pear from the bottom (a melon baller works well for this), and then cut a thin slice from the bottom so that the pear will stand upright. Carefully wrap each pear stem in a bit of aluminum foil so that the stems don't burn while roasting. Stand the pears in a 9-by-13-inch baking dish and pour the wine mixture over them. ❸ Place in the oven and roast for about 1¼ hours, or until tender when pierced with a knife, basting every 15 minutes with the wine sauce. ❹ Remove the pears from the oven and arrange on a serving platter or individual plates. Remove the vanilla bean from the sauce. Pour the remaining wine sauce into a saucepan over medium-high heat, bring to a simmer, and cook for 15 to 20 minutes, or until reduced to a syrupy glaze. Watch the sauce carefully to make sure it doesn't foam up and burn. Spoon the warm glaze over the pears. ❺ To serve, garnish with the mint leaves and serve the biscotti or ice cream alongside the pears, if desired. Serve warm or at room temperature.

Advance Preparation: Can be prepared up to 8 hours ahead through step 4 and kept at room temperature.

[SERVES 8]

This quintessential American bistro dessert uses the freshest seasonal fruits available and is a snap to prepare. Sometimes called a *galette* in French cooking, this free-form tart has countless variations. A favorite traditional version combines apples and pears in the cooler months. You can vary the spices, matching them with the fruits you choose. Make sure to adjust the amount of sugar according to the sweetness of the fruit. In this summer adaptation, the skin is deliberately left on the plums and peaches for a rustic texture.

❶ Prepare the crust: Place the flour, salt, and sugar in a food processor fitted with a metal blade and process for about 5 seconds. Add the butter and 2 to 3 tablespoons of the ice water and process for 5 to 10 seconds, or until you have a crumblike texture. If the mixture does not hold together when pressed between your fingertips, add a little more ice water and process briefly to continue. Pat the dough into a round for easy rolling.
❷ Select a 10-inch springform pan or a tart pan with a removable bottom. Remove the sides (you won't need them for this free-form tart) and place the bottom on a heavy baking sheet with a rim. On a floured work surface, roll out the pastry into a round 13 inches in diameter. Roll the pastry back onto the rolling pin and transfer it to the pan bottom, positioning it to cover the round, with a 3-inch border extending beyond the rim onto the baking sheet. Refrigerate while making the filling. ❸ Preheat the oven to 400 degrees F. Prepare the filling: In a bowl, combine 1 tablespoon of the sugar, 1 tablespoon of the flour, the plums, and the peaches. Stir gently to mix well. Remove the pan from the refrigerator and sprinkle 2 tablespoons sugar and the remaining 1 tablespoon flour evenly over the center of the crust. Arrange the fruit mixture in the center of the pastry, and then fold about 3 inches of the pastry edges up around the fruit, making pleats, to create a free-form tart. Brush the pastry rim with water and evenly sprinkle the remaining 2 tablespoons sugar over the fruit.
❹ Bake for 40 to 45 minutes, or until the fruit filling is bubbling and the crust is caramelized. Remove to a rack and let cool for at least 20 minutes. Transfer the tart to a round serving platter. Slice and serve with ice cream.

Advance Preparation: Can be made up to 8 hours ahead and kept at room temperature. Serve at room temperature or reheat in an oven at 325 degrees F for 10 to 15 minutes.

[SERVES 6]

Crust

1¼ cups all-purpose flour

¼ teaspoon salt

1 teaspoon sugar

½ cup unsalted butter, frozen, cut into
    small pieces

about ¼ cup ice water

Filling

5 tablespoons sugar

2 tablespoons all-purpose flour

3 medium or 2 large plums (Santa Rosas
    work nicely), unpeeled, pitted and cut
    into ½-inch pieces

3 medium or 2 large peaches, unpeeled,
    pitted and cut into ½-inch pieces

1 pint French vanilla ice cream (optional)

nectarine-cherry cobbler

The cobbler is an early American dessert that never seems to go out of fashion. It is basically a fruit mixture with a biscuit-style top crust, and its name comes from the cobbled effect created by the dough. You'll find that partially cooking the filling prior to adding the dough helps the dough cook more evenly.

Filling

10 nectarines or peaches, unpeeled, pitted
    and sliced into 1-inch pieces

3 cups pitted and halved cherries

3 tablespoons sugar

2 teaspoons finely chopped lemon zest

Dough

2 cups all-purpose flour

¼ cup plus 2 tablespoons sugar

1½ teaspoons baking powder

1 teaspoon baking soda

½ teaspoon salt

6 tablespoons chilled unsalted butter, cut
into small pieces

¾ cup plus 2 tablespoons buttermilk

1 teaspoon vanilla extract

1 large egg

1 pint French vanilla ice cream

❶ Preheat the oven to 400 degrees F. Butter and flour a 9-by-13-inch baking dish. ❷ Prepare the filling: In a bowl, combine the fruits, sugar, and lemon zest and stir gently to mix well. Spoon into the prepared dish. The fruit should come to within ¼ inch of the rim of the dish. (Save room for the cobbler dough.) Place the fruit mixture in the oven and bake for 20 minutes, or until hot and bubbly. ❸ Meanwhile, prepare the dough: In a bowl, combine the flour, ¼ cup sugar, baking powder, baking soda, and salt. Add the butter and cut it in with your fingers or two forks until it resembles the size of small peas. In a small bowl, combine the buttermilk, vanilla, and egg, and whisk to combine. Pour it into the center of the dough mixture, and mix to combine with a wooden spoon. The dough will be sticky. ❹ When the fruit has cooked for 20 minutes, remove it from the oven. Using an ice cream scoop, drop the dough onto the hot fruit. You can spread out the dough and make it as even as you like. The more uneven the dough, the more cobbled the dough will look. Sprinkle the remaining 2 tablespoons sugar over the dough and return the cobbler to the oven for 20 to 25 minutes longer, or until it is golden brown. ❺ Remove the cobbler from the oven and let cool for 30 minutes on a rack. Serve with vanilla ice cream. The cobbler is best served warm.

Advance Preparation: Can be prepared up to 8 hours ahead, covered, and kept at room temperature. Serve at room temperature or reheat in an oven at 325 degrees F for 10 to 15 minutes.

[SERVES 6 ➡ 8]

winter apple crisp with dried fruits

Fruit crisps have long been a part of America's dessert table, probably because they are so easy to prepare and offer homey comfort. This old-fashioned favorite uses dried cherries or cranberries (a relatively new discovery on the food scene) along with dried apricots to add a contrast in both color and flavor. Serve with a large scoop of French vanilla ice cream or frozen yogurt. This crisp has become a welcome addition to my Thanksgiving dessert menu.

❶ Preheat the oven to 350 degrees F. Butter a 9-by-13-inch baking dish. Set aside. ❷ Prepare the topping: Spread the pecans evenly on a baking sheet and toast in the oven for 5 to 7 minutes, or until they begin to change color and are fragrant. Watch carefully to be sure they do not burn. Remove to a plate and let cool. ❸ In a bowl, stir together the flour, cinnamon, nutmeg, allspice, cloves, and salt. Add the pecans, rolled oats, granulated sugar, brown sugar, and butter. Rub together all the ingredients between your fingertips until they are evenly distributed and the mixture is crumbly and resembles coarse bread crumbs. Set aside. ❹ Prepare the filling: Place the apples in a bowl and toss immediately with the lemon juice, dried cherries, and apricots. Be sure to coat the apples evenly with the lemon juice. Spoon the filling into the prepared dish and sprinkle the topping evenly over the fruit, pressing down lightly and leaving about ¼-inch space between the topping and the rim of the dish. ❺ Bake for 40 to 45 minutes, or until the topping is golden brown and bubbling. Cover with aluminum foil if the crust begins to overbrown. Remove from the oven and let cool for 15 minutes before serving.

Advance Preparation: Can be made up to 1 day ahead, covered, and refrigerated. Reheat, tented with foil, in an oven at 350 degrees F for 20 minutes.

[SERVES 6]

Topping

¾ cup coarsely chopped pecans

½ cup plus 2 tablespoons all-purpose flour

½ teaspoon ground cinnamon

¼ teaspoon freshly grated nutmeg

¼ teaspoon ground allspice

⅛ teaspoon ground cloves

pinch of salt

¾ cup old-fashioned rolled oats

⅓ cup granulated sugar

½ cup firmly packed dark brown sugar

½ cup plus 2 tablespoons chilled
    unsalted butter, cut into small pieces

Filling

8 Golden Delicious apples, about 4 pounds,
    peeled, cored, and cut into ½-inch-
    thick slices

3 tablespoons fresh lemon juice

½ cup dried pitted cherries or dried
    cranberries

½ cup sliced dried apricots

mixed berry bread pudding

This home-spun dessert made from leftover bread and rich custard has come a long way. Today's restaurant menus feature myriad adaptations such as gingerbread, white chocolate, and lemon, to name just a few. There is no definitive recipe. Served in soufflé dishes, in individual ramekins, or in a shallow baking dish, bread puddings are difficult to resist because of their old-fashioned quality.

Here, fresh, tart berries are paired with the sweet custard. The top becomes brown and crisp, while the inside remains moist with the texture of pudding. Use a good-quality bread such as challah, brioche, raisin bread, or even a sweet corn bread, and allow it to dry out for a day so that it will absorb the custard. You can do this by putting it out on the counter overnight, or in an oven at 250 degrees F for half an hour. It is also important to let the bread absorb the custard fully by allowing it to sit until you can feel that a cube is soaked through to the center. Lastly, a water bath is used to control the cooking temperature so that the custard does not overcook and curdle.

8 cups cubed (1-inch cubes) day-old challah

2 cups blueberries

1 cup raspberries

6 large whole eggs

2 large egg yolks

1¼ cups granulated sugar

3 cups milk

1 tablespoon vanilla extract

pinch of freshly grated nutmeg

boiling water, as needed

confectioners' sugar, for dusting

whipped cream, for garnish (optional)

❶ Grease a 9-by-13-inch glass baking dish. Arrange the bread and the berries in the dish, making sure that they are evenly distributed. ❷ In the bowl of an electric mixer, beat the whole eggs and egg yolks on medium speed until they are frothy. Add the sugar and beat until thick and lemon colored, about 3 minutes. Reduce the speed to low, add the milk, and mix to combine. Add the vanilla and nutmeg and mix to combine. ❸ Ladle the custard over the bread. Let the pudding sit for 30 minutes to 1 hour to help the bread absorb the custard, occasionally pushing the bread down with a wooden spoon. Meanwhile, preheat the oven to 375 degrees F. ❹ Place the baking dish in a larger baking pan. Pour almost-boiling water into the larger baking pan to reach halfway up the sides of the pudding dish. Place the pudding in the oven and bake for 40 to 45 minutes. ❺ Using long oven mitts to protect your hands, push the bread down with a large wooden spoon. The remaining liquid custard will rise to the surface. Spoon the custard evenly over the bread slices. Bake for about 10 minutes more, or until a skewer inserted into the center comes out clean. ❻ Remove the pudding from the oven and let rest on a rack for about 10 minutes. Using a fine-mesh sieve, dust the top with the confectioners' sugar. Serve in squares alone or with whipped cream. It is also excellent served cold the next day.

Advance Preparation: Can be prepared up to 4 hours ahead, covered, and left at room temperature. The pudding can also be made a day ahead and served chilled.

[SERVES 6 ➡ 8]

lemon meringue tart with macadamia crust

Macadamia nuts make this crust a little more delicate than most, so if the dough crumbles a bit when laying it in the tart pan, just press it together. Piped rosettes of meringue add an elegance that is not found in those big cloudlike namesakes perched under glass in your local diner.

Crust

1½ cups all-purpose flour

¼ cup macadamia nuts

pinch of salt

2 tablespoons confectioners' sugar

6 tablespoons frozen unsalted butter,
    cut into small pieces

1 tablespoon chilled vegetable shortening

1 large egg yolk

2½ tablespoons ice water

Filling

1 cup granulated sugar

6 tablespoons cornstarch

¼ teaspoon salt

2 cups water

4 large egg yolks, lightly beaten

3 tablespoons unsalted butter

½ cup fresh lemon juice, strained

finely chopped zest of 1 lemon

Meringue

5 large egg whites

¼ teaspoon cream of tartar

⅛ teaspoon salt

½ cup granulated sugar

❶ Prepare the crust: In a food processor fitted with the metal blade, combine the flour, nuts, salt, and confectioners' sugar. Process briefly to finely chop the nuts. Add the butter and shortening and process for 5 to 10 seconds, or until the mixture resembles coarse meal. With the motor running, add the egg yolk and ice water and process just until the dough begins to come together in a rough mass. ❷ Gather the dough into a ball and place on a lightly floured work surface. Press the dough into a round shape for easy rolling. Roll the dough into a circle large enough to fit a 10-inch tart pan with a removable bottom, adding flour as needed to prevent sticking. Drape the pastry over the rolling pin and fit it into the pan. Roll the pin over the pan with moderate pressure to remove excess overlapping dough. Press the pastry with your fingers so it adheres to the sides of the pan. Cover with plastic wrap and refrigerate for 2 hours. ❸ Preheat the oven to 350 degrees F. Prick the bottom and sides of the pastry with a fork. Line the tart with parchment paper or aluminum foil and fill with pie weights or dried beans. Bake until the crust is dry, about 20 minutes. Remove the weights or beans and paper or foil and return the crust to the oven. Bake for 8 to 10 minutes longer, or until golden. Transfer to a rack and let cool. ❹ Prepare the filling: Combine the granulated sugar, cornstarch, and salt in a heavy saucepan and whisk until well mixed and no lumps remain. Slowly drizzle in the water a little at a time, whisking constantly and never adding more water until the mixture is smooth. Stir in the yolks, whisking well to combine. ❺ Place the saucepan over medium heat and bring to a low boil stirring constantly with a wooden spoon. Be sure to run the spoon across the bottom and sides of the pan often. Alternate with a whisk to prevent lumps from forming. When the mixture reaches a boil (after 8 to 10 minutes), let boil for 1 minute while stirring. The custard should be very thick. Remove the pan from the heat, add the butter and gradually stir in the lemon juice until fully incorporated and the butter is melted. Stir in the lemon zest. Pour the hot filling into the cooled tart crust. ❻ Prepare the meringue: In a large bowl, using an electric mixer, beat the egg whites on medium speed for a few seconds. Add the cream of tartar and salt and continue beating for about 2 minutes, or until the egg whites hold soft peaks. Increase the speed to high and add the granulated sugar in a slow, steady stream, stopping occasionally to scrape down the sides of the bowl. Continue beating for 2 to 3 minutes, or until stiff peaks form. ❼ Gently scoop the meringue into a pastry bag fitted with a ¾-inch-wide plain or star tip and pipe large rosettes onto the tart, making circular rows to cover the filling completely. ❽ Place the tart in the oven and bake for 12 to 15 minutes, or until the meringue is golden and brown and firm to the touch, rotating a few times to promote even coloring. Transfer to a rack and let cool completely. Serve at room temperature or chilled.

Advance Preparation: Can be prepared up to 1 day ahead, covered, and refrigerated.

MAKES ONE 10-INCH TART [SERVES 6 ➡ 8]

pumpkin caramel flan

Here, pumpkin pie filling, an American favorite, is paired with a Mexican-style flan to solve the dessert dilemma on holiday tables and throughout the cooler months. This flan has all the components of a satisfying dessert, while actually being a bit lighter than the usual pies and rich desserts we associate with holiday indulgence. You can use regular evaporated milk or the skim version. Be sure to make the flan a day ahead so that the flavors have a chance to marry and the custard reaches its proper dense texture. If you want to make the flan in smaller ramekins, cook them for only half the time of the larger version.

Caramel

½ cup sugar

2 tablespoons water

Custard

1 cup canned pumpkin, unsweetened and
    without spices

1¼ cups sugar

1½ cups whole or skim evaporated milk

5 large eggs

2 teaspoons vanilla extract

1 teaspoon ground cinnamon

pinch of freshly grated nutmeg

pinch of ground allspice

❶ Preheat the oven to 350 degrees F. ❷ Prepare the caramel: Combine the sugar and water in a small, heavy saucepan. Do not use a dark-colored pan, or you will not be able to see the color of the caramel. Place over low heat to dissolve the sugar. Do not stir. Turn up the heat to medium-high and continually swirl the pan over the burner. The mixture will be bubbly. If sugar crystals form on the sides of the pan, cover it for 1 minute to dissolve them. Boil for 6 to 8 minutes, or until the mixture turns a golden brown. Watch carefully, as the caramel can burn easily, and if it is too dark, it will continue to cook and taste burnt. As soon as the caramel mixture turns golden brown, remove it from the heat. ❸ Pour the caramel into a 1½-quart porcelain baking dish (a 6-cup soufflé dish works well). Rotate the dish to spread the caramel evenly over the bottom of the dish. Don't worry if it is not even; it will distribute itself during the baking process. ❹ Prepare the custard: Place the pumpkin and sugar in a bowl and whisk in the milk until well mixed. Then add the eggs one at a time, whisking after each addition, until completely incorporated. Add the vanilla, cinnamon, nutmeg, and allspice and whisk to combine. Pour the mixture into the caramel-lined dish. Cover tightly with aluminum foil. ❺ Set the dish in a larger baking pan. Pour almost-boiling water into the larger pan to reach halfway up the sides of the flan dish. Transfer the dish in its water bath to the lower third of the oven. Be sure to regulate the oven so the water in the pan never heats above a simmer. Bake for 1¼ hours or until a tester inserted into the custard 1 inch from the outside edge comes out clean. Remove the baking pan from the oven and the flan dish from the water bath. Uncover and let cool to room temperature. Re-cover and refrigerate overnight or until well chilled. ❻ To unmold, run a knife carefully between the custard and the sides of the dish. Place a serving plate upside down over the dish, quickly invert the dish and plate together, and lift off the dish. Drizzle any caramel remaining in the dish over the top of the flan. If the caramel seems to be sticking to the bottom of the dish, place the dish in a skillet with simmering water to melt the hardened caramel. Cut the custard and serve each portion with a spoonful of the caramel.

Advance Preparation: Can be prepared up to 3 days ahead through step 5 and refrigerated.

[SERVES 6]

warm chocolate pudding cakes

These sophisticated pudding cakes require an excellent chocolate, such as bittersweet Vahlrona. You can make them up hours ahead of time and keep them refrigerated until just before baking. I like to dust them with confectioners' sugar as they come out of the oven, and accompany them with a dollop of crème fraîche or slightly softened vanilla ice cream. I've even served them chilled after they have been baked, and have received rave responses.

❶ Preheat the oven to 375 degrees F. Lightly butter six 1-cup ramekins. ❷ In the top of a double boiler over simmering water, combine the chocolate and butter. Heat until completely melted, stirring to blend. Remove from over the water and let cool for a few minutes. ❸ In a bowl, using an electric mixer, beat together the eggs, egg yolks, and sugar on medium speed for about 5 minutes, or until the mixture is a light lemon color. Add the flour, blending it in completely, and then add the cooled chocolate-butter mixture. Mix briefly just to blend. Fill each of the prepared ramekins half full. ❹ Bake for 11 to 12 minutes, or until each cake is set around the outside edges but the center trembles slightly when the ramekin is moved. (Watch carefully. If you overbake the cake it will be dry instead of creamy in the center.) Remove from the oven and, using a fine-mesh strainer, dust the tops with the confectioners' sugar. Serve on a dessert plate with a small scoop of ice cream or crème fraîche.

Advance Preparation: Can be prepared up to 4 hours ahead through step 3, lightly covered with aluminum foil or plastic wrap, and refrigerated. The cakes may need to cook a minute or two longer, since they are chilled.

[SERVES 6]

5 ½ ounces best-quality bittersweet
    chocolate, cut into small pieces
½ cup plus 1 tablespoon unsalted butter
3 large eggs
3 large egg yolks
⅓ cup granulated sugar
5 tablespoons all-purpose flour

Garnish

confectioners' sugar for dusting
French vanilla ice cream or crème fraîche

heath bar chocolate chip cookies

When I was a child, there was no question that if I had my choice of any candy, the all-American Heath Bar always won out. Here, I've added that wonderful toffee-chocolate brittle to America's favorite cookie to give it an underlying buttery flavor. Combined with the oats, these cookies have a crisp, crunchy texture. If you prefer larger cookies, drop golf ball–sized spheres onto baking sheets and bake a few minutes longer.

1 ¾ cups all-purpose flour

½ cup old-fashioned rolled oats

1 teaspoon baking soda

1 teaspoon salt

1 cup unsalted butter, room temperature

1 cup firmly packed dark brown sugar

½ cup granulated sugar

1 teaspoon vanilla extract

2 large eggs

1 ½ cups semisweet chocolate chips

2 packages (1.4 ounces each) Heath Bars,
    finely crushed (about ½ cup)

¾ cup chopped walnuts or pecans

❶ Preheat the oven to 375 degrees F. ❷ In a small bowl, combine the flour, oats, baking soda, and salt and mix well. In a large bowl, beat together the butter, brown sugar, granulated sugar, and vanilla until creamy. Add the eggs one at a time, beating well after each addition. Add the flour mixture a little at a time and beat until incorporated after each addition. Stir in the chocolate chips, crushed Heath Bars, and nuts. ❸ Drop the dough teaspoonfuls onto ungreased baking sheets, spacing them 2 inches apart. ❹ Bake for 9 to 11 minutes, or until golden, rotating the baking sheet 180 degrees halfway through the baking. Remove from the oven and let the cookies cool on the sheets for 2 minutes. Transfer the cookies to racks to cool completely.

Advance Preparation: Can be stored in airtight containers for up to 1 week, or frozen for up to 1 month.

[MAKES ABOUT 5 DOZEN 2½-INCH COOKIES]

chocolate celebration cake

Chocoholics used to turn to Europe to satisfy their cravings for sweets, but America created its own little indulgence: the chocolate chip. Legend has it that in the 1930s, a resourceful restaurateur in Massachusetts chopped up a chocolate bar, tossed the broken bits into cookie dough, and the little chips caught on in New England. Today, America's love affair with chocolate chips has grown beyond just cookies.

Here, adding chocolate chips to the batter enriches the texture, to make this truly sumptuous cake even moister. The two layers of dark chocolate are offset by whipped cream, with a sprinkling of confectioners' sugar on the top layer for an elegant finale. This cake is so pretty that even a novice baker can feel like an accomplished pastry chef when serving it. To make the cake even fancier, add chocolate shavings to the whipped cream sides, or pipe whipped cream rosettes around the top layer. An extra bonus is that this cake tastes almost as moist the second day as on the first.

❶ Preheat the oven to 350 degrees F. Butter and flour two 9-inch round cake pans. ❷ Prepare the cake: In a bowl, sift together the flour, sugar, baking soda, and salt. ❸ Place the cocoa in a large bowl and slowly add the hot water while stirring constantly. When the mixture is smooth, stir in the cold water. Stir in the vegetable oil and vanilla. Whisk in the flour mixture just until incorporated. Pour the batter into the prepared cake pans, dividing it evenly, and sprinkle the chocolate chips evenly over the pan. ❹ Bake the cakes for 30 to 35 minutes, or until they begin to come away from the sides of the pans and the tops are springy to the touch. Remove to racks to cool for 20 minutes. Run a thin-bladed knife around the edges of the pans to loosen the cakes, then invert onto the racks to cool completely before assembling. ❺ Meanwhile, prepare the frosting: In the bowl, using an electric mixer on medium speed, whip together the cream and 2 tablespoons of the confectioners' sugar until very stiff peaks form. ❻ Place the first cake layer, chocolate chip side up, on a serving plate. Spread half of the whipped cream over the layer, leaving a ½-inch border around the edges. Top with the second cake layer, chocolate chip side up, and push down gently so that the whipped cream spreads to the edges. Using a long rubber spatula, spread the remaining whipped cream around the sides of the cake, making old-fashioned peaks. ❼ Using a fine-mesh strainer, evenly dust the top of the cake with the remaining 1 tablespoon confectioners' sugar.

Advance Preparation: Can be prepared up to 1 day ahead, covered, and refrigerated. Remove from the refrigerator 30 minutes before serving.

MAKES ONE 9-INCH, 2-LAYER CAKE [SERVES 8 ➡ 10]

Cake

3 cups all-purpose flour, sifted

2 cups granulated sugar

2 teaspoons baking soda

½ teaspoon salt

½ cup unsweetened cocoa powder

1 cup hot water

1 cup cold water

1 cup vegetable oil

1 teaspoon vanilla extract

1 cup semisweet chocolate chips

Frosting

2 cups (1 pint) whipping cream

3 tablespoons confectioners' sugar

pumpkin ice cream pie with gingersnap crust

Pumpkin plays an important role in American bistro recipes because this member of the gourd family has been a part of American cooking from the earliest days. Pumpkin lends itself to being updated from classic dishes to creatively casual desserts. For this reason, I couldn't resist including two pumpkin desserts, each with its own unique style. The first time I added this to my holiday repertoire, the decision was unanimous to keep this ice cream pie on the menu every year. I've found that freezing the pie shell, unmolding it, and then replacing it in the pie plate makes it easy to cut perfect slices that don't stick to the plate.

Crust

2 tablespoons finely chopped pecans

1½ cups gingersnap crumbs (from 25 gingersnap cookies)

6 tablespoons unsalted butter, melted

Filling

½ cup firmly packed dark brown sugar

1 teaspoon pumpkin pie seasoning, or ¼ teaspoon each ground cinnamon, freshly grated nutmeg, ground ginger, and allspice

1 cup canned pumpkin, unsweetened and without spices

1 quart good-quality French vanilla ice cream, softened in the refrigerator

16 pecan halves

1 recipe Caramel Sauce (page 155)

❶ Preheat the oven to 375 degrees F. Line a 9-by-2-inch-deep pie plate tightly with aluminum foil. Mix the pecans and gingersnap crumbs together in a bowl. Add the butter and toss the crumbs to blend well. Press the crumbs evenly over the bottom and sides of the pie plate, using the back of a spoon, the heel of your hand, or your fingers. Chill until firm, about 30 minutes. ❷ Bake the crust for 6 minutes. Remove to a rack and let cool. ❸ Place the crust in the freezer for 2 hours to chill. Remove from the freezer and unmold the pie shell onto a flat surface. Peel the foil away very carefully so the shell stays intact, then replace the shell directly into the pie plate. ❹ Prepare the filling: Combine the brown sugar and the pumpkin pie seasoning in a large bowl. Stir in the pumpkin with a large spoon, making sure it is smooth. Add the softened ice cream by big spoonfuls, beating in each addition until there are no lumps. Mix until thoroughly combined. ❺ Spoon the ice cream into the prepared crust. Place in the freezer and freeze for 1 hour. Remove from the freezer and arrange the pecan halves around the outside edge of the pie in a circle, pushing them down so that they are embedded in the ice cream mixture. Return to the freezer and freeze a few more hours. When frozen, cover tightly. ❻ To serve, thaw slightly in the refrigerator for 30 minutes and cut into slices. You will need a metal spatula to ease the pie slices out of the pan. Serve with the warm Caramel Sauce.

Advance Preparation: Can be prepared up to 2 weeks ahead, well covered, and frozen. Thaw slightly in the refrigerator for 30 minutes before serving.

[SERVES 8 ➡ 10]

ultimate ice cream sundae

Combining ice cream and toppings has been an American classic for years, along with ice cream parlors and drugstore fountains. Frozen yogurt often serves as a low-fat substitute these days, but nothing compares to an old-fashioned ice cream sundae with the works. Scoop your favorite ice cream into sundae dishes, spoon Hot Fudge Sauce and Caramel Sauce over the top, and finish it off with toasted nuts. There is nothing finer.

❶ Preheat the oven to 350 degrees F. Spread the nuts evenly on a baking sheet and toast in the oven for 5 to 7 minutes, or until they begin to change color and are fragrant. Watch carefully to be sure they do not burn. Set the nuts aside. ❷ Prepare the Hot Fudge Sauce: Combine the cream and sugar in a heavy saucepan over medium heat and stir until the sugar dissolves, about 2 minutes. Add the chocolates, butter, and salt, and stir until smooth and completely melted, about 2 more minutes. Bring the mixture to a simmer over medium heat, stirring constantly. Add the corn syrup and vanilla, and cook for 1 minute while stirring constantly. Remove the pan from the heat and cover to keep warm. ❸ Prepare the Caramel Sauce: Combine the sugar and water in a heavy saucepan. Do not use a dark-colored pan, or you will not be able to see the color of the caramel. Place over low heat to dissolve the sugar. Turn up the heat and continually swirl the pan over the burner. Do not stir. The mixture will be bubbly. If sugar crystals form on the sides of the pan, cover it for 1 minute to dissolve them. Boil for 6 to 8 minutes, or until the mixture turns a golden brown. Watch carefully, as the caramel can burn easily, and if it is too dark, it will continue to cook and taste burnt. As soon as the caramel mixture turns golden brown, remove from the heat and let it cool down for about 3 minutes, making sure it is still liquid. Return the caramel sauce to low heat and stir in the cream and vanilla, stirring constantly to create a caramel sauce. The mixture may look separated, but if you continue to stir, it will become smooth after about 2 minutes. Remove from the heat and cover to keep warm. ❹ Scoop the ice cream into chilled bowls and ladle the warm sauces over the top. Sprinkle with the toasted nuts and serve immediately.

Advance Preparation: The sauces can be made up to 1 week ahead, covered, and refrigerated. Slowly reheat the sauces separately in the top of a double boiler over simmering water.

MAKES 1½ CUPS HOT FUDGE SAUCE AND 1½ CUPS CARAMEL SAUCE [SERVES 6 ➡ 8]

¼ cup pecan pieces or slivered blanched almonds

Hot Fudge Sauce
½ cup whipping cream

½ cup sugar

2 ounces unsweetened chocolate, chopped

3 ounces German's sweetened chocolate, chopped

3 tablespoons unsalted butter

pinch of salt

2 tablespoons light corn syrup

1 teaspoon vanilla extract

Caramel Sauce
1 cup sugar

½ cup water

1 cup whipping cream

2 teaspoons vanilla extract

1 quart French vanilla ice cream

Breakfast and Brunch Dishes

apple spiced streusel coffee cake

Studded with moist apple nuggets and topped with a golden crispy streusel, this coffee cake will adapt to whatever brunch menu you're serving. I prefer to bake it in a lightweight bundt pan because it cooks more evenly, but a 9-by-13-inch baking dish can be used.

Streusel

½ cup brown sugar

½ teaspoon ground ginger

½ teaspoon ground cinnamon

½ cup all-purpose flour

¼ cup cold unsalted butter, cut into
    small pieces

½ cup finely chopped walnuts

Cake

2¼ cups all-purpose flour

1½ teaspoons ground cinnamon

½ teaspoon freshly grated nutmeg

½ teaspoon ground ginger

1 teaspoon baking powder

1 teaspoon baking soda

½ teaspoon salt

½ cup unsalted butter, room temperature

¾ cup firmly packed dark brown sugar

½ cup granulated sugar

3 large eggs

2 apples, such as Granny Smith or
    Golden Delicious, peeled, cored,
    and roughly chopped

1¼ cups buttermilk, mixed with
    2 teaspoons vanilla extract

confectioners' sugar, for dusting

❶ Preheat the oven to 350 degrees F. Butter and flour a 10-cup bundt pan or a 9-by-13-inch baking dish. ❷ Prepare the streusel: In a bowl, combine the brown sugar, ginger, cinnamon, flour, and butter. Rub together all the ingredients between your fingertips until they are evenly distributed and the mixture resembles large bread crumbs. Mix in the walnuts, cover, and refrigerate until ready to use. ❸ Prepare the cake: In a large bowl, stir together the flour, cinnamon, nutmeg, ginger, baking powder, baking soda, and salt. ❹ In another bowl, using an electric mixer on medium speed, beat the butter until light and fluffy. Gradually add the sugars, continuing to beat until very light. Add the eggs one at a time, beating well each addition until fully incorporated. (Don't overbeat or the cake will be tough.) Gently stir in the chopped apples. ❺ With the mixer on low speed, alternately beat in the flour mixture and the buttermilk, in 2 batches, ending with the buttermilk and beating until just mixed. ❻ Spoon half of the batter into the prepared pan and sprinkle with one-third of the streusel. Spoon on the remaining batter, using a rubber spatula to smooth it into an even layer. Sprinkle the remaining streusel evenly over the top. Pat the streusel down gently. ❼ Bake for 40 to 45 minutes, or until the top of the cake is firm, the streusel is crisp and golden brown, and a tester inserted into the center of the cake comes out clean. Remove to a rack and let cool in the pan for 15 minutes. If using a bundt pan, invert the cake onto the rack and then invert it back onto a serving platter so that the streusel side is on top. Using a fine-mesh strainer, dust with confectioners' sugar and serve warm.

Advance Preparation: Can be prepared up to 1 day ahead, covered, and kept at room temperature.

[SERVES 8 ➡ 10]

cranberry-orange cornmeal muffins

Cranberries and yellow cornmeal team up for added texture and pure American flavor. These rustic, crusty muffins, crowned with a brown sugar crust, are wonderful served warm, accompanied with berry preserves. They are best eaten the day they are made.

❶ Preheat the oven to 350 degrees F. Generously butter the cups of a 12-cup muffin tin. ❷ In a large mixing bowl, combine the baking powder, salt, flour, and cornmeal, and set aside. Combine the milk and orange juice in a measuring cup and set aside. ❸ In another bowl, using an electric mixer on medium speed, beat the butter until it is light and fluffy. Gradually add the granulated sugar and beat for about 2 minutes, or until very light. Add the eggs one at a time, beating after each addition until completely incorporated. Add the vanilla and orange zest and mix well. Using a spatula, fold in half of the flour mixture, and then half of the milk mixture. Repeat with the remaining flour mixture and milk mixture. Fold in the cranberries. ❹ Scoop the batter into the prepared tin, dividing it evenly and making sure to get an equal amount of cranberries into each one. Evenly sprinkle the brown sugar over the top of each muffin. Bake the muffins for 30 minutes, or until golden. Cool on a rack for a few minutes, then unmold and serve warm or at room temperature.

[MAKES 12 MUFFINS]

2 teaspoons baking powder

¼ teaspoon salt

1½ cups all-purpose flour

½ cup yellow cornmeal

¼ cup milk

¼ cup fresh orange juice

½ cup unsalted butter, room temperature

¾ cup granulated sugar

2 large eggs

1 teaspoon vanilla extract

2 teaspoons finely chopped orange zest

1 cup plus 2 tablespoons dried cranberries

2 tablespoons brown sugar

golden raisin–bran muffins

These light muffins taste great any time of day. Although some bran muffins can be dry, soaking the bran cereal with the liquid ingredients is the secret to keeping these moist. Here apple sauce has replaced part of the oil with excellent results. Make sure to select unprocessed bran, like All Bran or Bran Buds, for best results. Do not use bran flakes.

2 large eggs

½ cup firmly packed brown sugar

¼ cup vegetable oil

¼ cup applesauce

2 cups buttermilk

½ teaspoon salt

*1¾ cups wheat bran cereal (see
    recipe introduction)*

2 cups all-purpose flour

2 teaspoons baking soda

¾ cup golden raisins

❶ Preheat the oven to 400 degrees F. Generously butter the cups of a 12-cup muffin tin. ❷ In a large bowl, combine the eggs, brown sugar, vegetable oil, apple sauce, buttermilk, salt, and bran cereal. Mix well with a wooden spoon. Let rest for at least 10 minutes to soften the bran. ❸ In another bowl, stir together the flour and baking soda. Stir in the bran mixture and mix until just combined. Stir in the raisins. ❹ Scoop the batter into the prepared tin, dividing it evenly. Bake for 20 minutes, or until golden. Do not overcook or they will be dry. Cool on a rack for a few minutes, then unmold and serve warm or at room temperature.

Advance Preparation: Can be prepared up to 1 day ahead, stored in a plastic bag, and kept at room temperature. Reheat in an oven at 350 degrees F for 10 minutes before serving.

[MAKES 12 MUFFINS]

banana buttermilk pancakes
with banana-orange compote

These old-fashioned buttermilk pancakes are lightly spiced with cinnamon and flavored with puréed banana. A fragrant compote accompanies the fluffy cakes in place of the more common maple syrup. Serve the pancakes with your favorite grilled breakfast meats such as turkey sausages or apple-smoked bacon. Big bowls of cappuccino finish off this satisfying breakfast menu.

❶ Prepare the compote: In a large skillet, melt the butter over medium heat. Add the bananas and sauté for about 1 minute, or until just beginning to soften. Add the brown sugar, orange juice, and cinnamon, and bring to a boil. Boil for 1 minute, or until slightly thickened. Remove from the heat, cover, and reserve. ❷ Prepare the batter: In a large bowl, stir together the flour, sugar, baking powder, baking soda, cinnamon, and salt, mixing well. ❸ In a large measuring cup, combine the buttermilk, egg, and melted butter and whisk with a fork until well combined. Add the mashed banana and blend it in well. Don't worry if the mixture is still a little lumpy. ❹ Add the buttermilk mixture to the flour mixture and mix together with a fork or a whisk until you have a smooth batter. (You can also use a hand blender if you like a smooth consistency.) Return the batter to the measuring cup for easy pouring. ❺ Heat a griddle or large nonstick skillet over medium-high heat until a drop of water flicked onto the surface skitters across and then disappears. Lightly oil the surface with some of the vegetable oil. Pour a scant ¼ cup of the batter onto the surface for each pancake. Cook for 3 to 5 minutes, depending on the pan and the heat, or until little bubbles appear on the surface of the pancake. Using a sharp-edged spatula, turn the pancakes and cook on the other side for 1 to 2 minutes, or until both sides are equally browned. Transfer to a platter in an oven at 200 degrees F to keep warm while you finish cooking the rest of the batter, adding more oil to the griddle or skillet as needed. ❻ To serve, spoon the warm fruit compote over the pancakes. Serve immediately.

Advance Preparation: Can be made up to 3 hours ahead through step 4. Refrigerate the batter until ready to use.

[SERVES 4 ➡ 6]

Banana-Orange Compote

1 tablespoon unsalted butter

2 bananas, cut into ½-inch-thick slices

1 tablespoon brown sugar

½ cup fresh orange juice

¼ teaspoon ground cinnamon

Pancake Batter

1 cup all-purpose flour

1 tablespoon sugar

1 teaspoon baking powder

½ teaspoon baking soda

½ teaspoon ground cinnamon

¼ teaspoon salt

1 ¼ cups buttermilk

1 large egg

2 tablespoons unsalted butter, melted

1 ripe banana, peeled and mashed

1 tablespoon vegetable oil

sticky buns

In Southern Californian beach towns, early morning joggers and surfers line up outside tiny outlets for postworkout cinnamon buns. In the windy city, Chicagoans head to Swedish bakeries for gooey sticky buns. And in Seattle, neighborhood coffee shops hold competitions to determine who bakes the best cinnamon rolls in the Pacific Northwest. These gooey sticky buns with chopped pecans could compete with the best. Putting them together takes a little time, but you can prepare the dough the night before and let it rise overnight to bake first thing in the morning.

4 ½ cups all-purpose flour

1 package active dry yeast

1¼ cups milk (do not use nonfat)

¼ cup sugar

½ cup unsalted butter, cut into 6 pieces

1 teaspoon salt

2 large eggs

Filling

¼ cup plus 2 tablespoons chopped pecans

¼ cup plus 2 tablespoons firmly packed brown sugar

1 teaspoon ground cinnamon

Topping

¾ cup firmly packed brown sugar

6 tablespoons unsalted butter, melted

2 tablespoons corn syrup

¾ cup chopped pecans

6 tablespoons unsalted butter, room temperature

❶ In a bowl, combine 1½ cups of the flour with the yeast. In a small saucepan over low heat, warm together the milk, sugar, butter, and salt, stirring occasionally, for 2 to 3 minutes, or until just warm and the butter is melted. Remove from the heat and let cool to lukewarm. ❷ Add the lukewarm milk mixture to the flour mixture along with the eggs. Using a mixer fitted with the paddle attachment, beat on low speed for 30 seconds, stopping as needed to scrape down the sides of the bowl. Increase the speed to high and beat for 3 minutes. Using a wooden spoon, stir in as much of the remaining 3 cups flour as possible. Turn out the dough onto a lightly floured surface. Knead in the remaining flour for 2 to 3 minutes, or until the dough is soft. ❸ Shape the dough into a ball and place in a lightly greased bowl, turning the ball once to coat. Cover the bowl with a towel and let the dough rise in a warm place until it doubles, at least 2 hours or as long as overnight. ❹ Meanwhile, prepare the filling: In a food processor fitted with the metal blade, combine all the filling ingredients and pulse until the pecans are finely chopped. Set aside. Butter a 9-by-13-inch glass baking dish. ❺ Prepare the topping: Combine the brown sugar, melted butter, and corn syrup in a bowl, whisking to blend well. Spread the mixture in the bottom of the prepared baking dish coating evenly. Sprinkle the pecans over the top. ❻ Punch down the dough and knead again briefly on a lightly floured surface. Divide the dough in half, and shape each half into a ball. Place the 2 balls back in the greased bowl, cover, and let rest for 10 minutes. ❼ On a lightly floured surface, roll out half of the dough into a 10-by-12-inch rectangle. Use the edge of a ruler to keep the sides straight. Spread with 3 tablespoons of the room-temperature butter. Sprinkle half of the filling mixture over the rectangle. Starting with the short side, roll up the rectangle like a jelly roll and brush water on the end to seal it at the seam. Make a second roll with the remaining dough, butter, and filling. ❽ Slice each dough roll crosswise into 6 equal pieces. Arrange all 12 pieces, cut side down, in the prepared baking dish. Cover loosely with a towel and let rise for 1 hour. Meanwhile, preheat the oven to 350 degrees F. ❾ Bake the rolls for 25 minutes, or until light brown. Remove the baking dish from the oven, place waxed paper over the rolls, and invert the dish onto a baking sheet to release the buns and topping. Use a knife to separate the buns from one another and allow the topping to drip down the sides. Serve warm.

Advance Preparation: Can be prepared up to 8 hours ahead through step 3.

[MAKES 12 ROLLS]

granola with maple-yogurt swirl

Granola came into vogue during the health-food movement of the 1960s, quietly retreated, and now it's back in fashion. Upscale bakeries sell house versions, each with its own mix of nuts, fruits, and grains. This homemade granola has a wonderful, toasted flavor with just a hint of honey—a perfect start to the weekend. Add any combination of dried fruits and nuts and make extra batches to toss into cookies and sprinkle over ice cream. During the summer months, heap mounds of fresh berries over the granola and yogurt for a truly pleasurable breakfast.

❶ Preheat the oven to 350 degrees F. In a large bowl, combine the oats, sunflower seeds, bran, pecans and almonds. Drizzle with the vegetable oil and toss well to coat evenly. ❷ In a small saucepan over low heat, warm the honey for 3 to 5 minutes, or until it liquefies. Drizzle the honey over the oat mixture and toss again to coat evenly. ❸ Divide the mixture evenly between two 11-by-17-inch baking sheets, spreading it out evenly. Bake for 15 minutes. Remove from the oven, stir the granola well, and spread it out again. Reduce the oven temperature to 325 degrees F, return the granola to the oven, and bake for 15 to 20 minutes longer, or until evenly browned, stirring twice. ❹ Remove the pans from the oven and let the granola cool completely. Stir in the cranberries. ❺ Meanwhile, prepare the Maple-Yogurt Swirl: In a small bowl, stir together the yogurt and maple syrup. Cover and refrigerate. ❻ To serve, pour the granola into bowls and top with the maple-yogurt mixture.

Advance Preparation: The granola can be stored in an airtight container for up to 2 weeks.

[MAKES 8 CUPS]

5 cups old-fashioned rolled oats

1½ cups unsalted sunflower seeds

1 cup wheat bran or oat bran

1 cup coarsely chopped pecans

½ cup sliced almonds

3 tablespoons vegetable oil

½ cup honey

⅔ cup dried cranberries

Maple-Yogurt Swirl

4 cups nonfat plain yogurt

6 tablespoons maple syrup

corned beef and cabbage hash

The word *hash* comes from the French *hacher*, "to chop." Corned beef hash had become so popular in America by the mid-nineteenth century that diners and lunch counters offering some form of the dish on their menus were nicknamed hash houses. One variation on this dish is red flannel hash, which is made by adding 2 or 3 cooked, peeled, and cubed beets (page 178) to the mixture along with the corned beef.

The next time you make corned beef and cabbage, reserve a cabbage quarter and 3 cups of corned beef for this American classic. Adding the briny flavors of cooked cabbage brings in a bold flavor dimension. The key to making this dish delicious is to stir it frequently after the first 10 minutes of cooking. That way the hash will become brown and crusty. Garnish these little ramekins with sprigs of fresh parsley for an elegant touch. I like to serve the hash for brunch with scrambled eggs or poached eggs.

2 pounds white or red potatoes, peeled and cut into ¼-inch cubes

3 cups cubed (¼-inch cubes) cooked corned beef

¼ cooked cabbage, finely chopped

½ cup whipping cream

2 tablespoons finely chopped parsley

1 teaspoon Worcestershire sauce

½ teaspoon salt

freshly ground black pepper

2 tablespoons vegetable oil

1 large onion, finely chopped

parsley sprigs, for garnish

❶ Bring a large pot of lightly salted water to a boil. Add the potatoes, and boil for 7 to 10 minutes, or until cooked but still slightly resistant when pierced with a fork. Drain well. ❷ In a large bowl, combine the potatoes, the corned beef, cabbage, cream, parsley, Worcestershire sauce, salt, and pepper. Mix well. ❸ In a 12½-inch nonstick skillet, heat the vegetable oil over medium heat. Add the onion and sauté, stirring occasionally, for 4 to 5 minutes, or until softened. Add the potato mixture to the onions and mix well to distribute the onions evenly. ❹ Spread the corned beef hash evenly in the skillet, flattening with a spatula as it cooks. Cook over medium-high heat for about 10 minutes, or until a slight crust forms on the bottom. Occasionally run the spatula around the edges or the skillet to keep the potatoes from sticking. Turn the mixture over and continue cooking, stirring frequently to break up the hash, for about 14 more minutes, or until crusty and browned. ❺ Spoon the mixture into six 1-cup ramekins, dividing it evenly. If you are serving this with eggs, keep the ramekins warm, uncovered, in an oven at 200 degrees F while you prepare the eggs. Alternatively, you can mold the hash in a ramekin and then turn out each serving onto an individual plate. Garnish with the parsley sprigs.

Advance Preparation: Can be prepared up to 2 days ahead, covered, and refrigerated. Reheat in a skillet over medium heat.

[SERVES 8]

stirred eggs with fresh herbs

These creamy scrambled eggs can be flavored in a variety of different ways: caviar and crème fraîche, tomatoes and fresh basil, sautéed mushrooms, sharp Cheddar cheese, prosciutto, or chopped Italian parsley. You can double or triple this recipe for a crowd, keeping in mind that you will need a large, deep skillet and the cooking time will be longer.

Straining the eggs before cooking them rids them of the albumen that sometimes causes them to be tough. Serve with your favorite crisp bacon or grilled sausages, along with thick slices of toasted French bread and your favorite preserves.

❶ In a bowl, whisk the eggs to combine. Put a fine-mesh strainer over another bowl and pour the eggs through it, making sure that the albumen remains in the strainer. Add the cream, salt, and pepper to the eggs and stir to combine. ❷ In a saucepan, melt the butter over medium heat. Add the eggs and stir continuously with a wooden spoon. When the eggs begin to form curds, keep stirring for 4 to 5 minutes, or until creamy but not dry, or until the desired consistency is reached. Fold in any flavoring (see recipe introduction) just before the eggs have finished cooking. ❸ Turn the eggs into a shallow bowl and garnish with the chives and parsley. Serve immediately.

[SERVES 3 OR 4]

8 large eggs
2 tablespoons whipping cream
salt and freshly ground black pepper
1 tablespoon unsalted butter

Garnish

1 tablespoon finely chopped chives
1 tablespoon finely chopped parsley

baked eggs with oven-roasted ratatouille

Ratatouille is often served as a first course or as an accompaniment to a main course. Here, it is transformed into a vegetable hash and topped with baked eggs. This dish is prepared in ramekins, which make a pretty presentation for a special occasion. A sprinkling of Parmesan cheese gives the eggs a hint of golden color. Begin with a sparkling wine cooler made with orange juice and cranberry juice. A basket of muffins and sliced fresh fruit on the table completes this American bistro brunch.

4½ cups Oven-Roasted Ratatouille
    (page 124)

6 large eggs

salt and freshly ground black pepper

2 tablespoons freshly grated Parmesan
    cheese

2 tablespoons finely chopped parsley

❶ Preheat the oven to 350 degrees F. Arrange six 1-cup round ramekins on a baking sheet and lightly spray the insides with nonstick cooking spray, or butter lightly. ❷ Heat the ratatouille in a saucepan over medium heat, or in the oven, until it is hot. Place ¾ cup of hot ratatouille in each ramekin, pressing down each slightly to make an even layer which covers the bottom completely. ❸ Break an egg into each ramekin, and sprinkle with salt and pepper. Bake for 20 minutes. ❹ Meanwhile, combine the cheese and parsley in a small bowl. ❺ After 20 minutes, sprinkle the cheese mixture evenly over the top of each egg. Continue baking for 2 to 3 more minutes, or until the egg is just set. Remove the ramekins from the oven and let them sit for a minute. The egg will set up a bit more after being removed from the oven. Serve immediately.

Advance Preparation: The ratatouille can be made 1 day ahead, covered, and refrigerated. Reheat just before using.

[SERVES 6]

This flat, round omeletlike pancake is highly adaptable. It can be served warm out of the oven, at room temperature, or chilled, each resulting in its own distinctive character. Frittatas can be as simple as adding some fresh herbs and cheese to beaten eggs or as complicated as you would like. Some filling variations include sautéed eggplant, asparagus, summer squash, broccoli, leeks, potatoes, cooked pasta, and bell peppers. If you prefer a different cheese, Gruyère or Parmesan works nicely. Serve with a basket of Cranberry-Orange Cornmeal Muffins (page 159) or Apple Spiced Streusel Coffee Cake (page 158).

❶ Preheat the oven to 425 degrees F. ❷ In an 11-inch nonstick skillet with an ovenproof handle (or cover a wooden handle with foil), heat the oil over medium heat. Add the shallots and sauté for about 2 minutes, or until softened but not brown. Raise the heat to medium-high, add the mushrooms, and sauté for 3 to 4 minutes, stirring constantly to coat the mushrooms with the shallots. Add the spinach leaves, cover, and continue cooking for 2 to 3 minutes, or until the leaves begin to wilt. Uncover and raise the heat to high for a minute to evaporate the excess moisture. Season with the salt and pepper. ❸ Combine the eggs, salt, and pepper in a bowl, and whisk until well blended. Stir in 1½ cups of the cheese. ❹ Flatten the vegetable ingredients in the skillet and pour the egg mixture over them. Cook over medium-low heat, stirring occasionally, for about 7 minutes, or until bottom is lightly set and cooked. Arrange the sliced tomatoes along the edge of the pan in a circular pattern. Sprinkle with the remaining ½ cup cheese. ❺ Transfer the skillet to the oven and bake for 10 to 15 minutes, or until the frittata is puffed and brown. Have 2 large (at least 12 inches in diameter) round platters ready. Remove the skillet from the oven and invert the frittata onto a platter, placing a spatula underneath it to ensure it will slide out easily. Invert again onto the other platter, so the puffed, browned surface faces up. (You can also serve this right out of the skillet.) ❻ To serve, arrange the sour cream in a mound in the center of the frittata and garnish with the salsa and parsley.

Advance Preparation: Can be made up to 1 day ahead through step 2, covered, and refrigerated. Bring to room temperature before continuing. You will need to add a tablespoon of butter or oil to the pan when continuing.

[SERVES 6]

2 tablespoons olive oil
2 shallots, finely chopped
½ pound fresh mushrooms, thinly sliced
1 bunch spinach, cleaned and stemmed
salt and freshly ground black pepper
12 large eggs
2 cups shredded sharp Cheddar or
    Jack cheese
3 plum tomatoes, sliced

Garnish
½ cup sour cream
½ cup fresh tomato salsa or Tomatillo
    Salsa (page 183)
2 tablespoons finely chopped parsley

summer picnic sandwich

This is a serious sandwich: big, hearty, and full of flavor. Prepare a Lemon-Rosemary Roasted Chicken ahead of time and slice the breast meat for the filling. Wrapping the loaf in butcher paper and tying off individual sandwiches with raffia makes an ideal—and impressive—lunch for picnics and summer outings where the meal has to travel. Variations on the filling include roasted red peppers, eggplant, zucchini, grilled lamb, sun-dried tomatoes, mozzarella cheese, and watercress.

1 French or sourdough baguette

½ cup Herb Vinaigrette (page 176)

1 small cucumber, peeled and thinly sliced

2 tomatoes, thinly sliced

12 large fresh basil leaves

breast meat from Lemon-Rosemary Roasted Chicken (page 74), thinly sliced

¾ cup drained, marinated artichoke hearts (6-ounce jar)

3 ounces fresh goat cheese

❶ Slice the baguette horizontally so that two-thirds of the bread is on the bottom half and one-third is on the top half. Scoop out most of the soft bread inside, leaving the thick crust with only a thin layer of bread. ❷ To assemble the sandwich: Brush some vinaigrette on the bottom half of the baguette. Top with cucumber slices, tomato slices, basil leaves, chicken slices, and artichoke hearts, distributing the ingredients evenly. Sprinkle with more vinaigrette. Top with the goat cheese. Cover with the top piece of bread and press down firmly. Wrap in plastic wrap and refrigerate for at least 2 hours. ❸ Remove the plastic wrap from the sandwich. Wrap the loaf in butcher paper. Wrap twine or raffia tightly around the loaf at 2-inch intervals. When ready to serve, using a sharp, serrated knife, slice through the bread between the twine ties to make individual sandwiches.

Advance Preparation: Can be prepared up to 8 hours ahead, covered, and refrigerated.

[SERVES 8]

Basics ⑩

turkey or chicken stock

This light-colored stock is rich in flavor. Store it in your freezer in 1- and 2-cup containers.

*4 pounds turkey or chicken necks
    and backs*

3 stalks celery

3 carrots, peeled and cut into halves

2 onions, cut into halves

*2 leeks, white and light green parts only,
    cleaned and sliced*

bouquet garni (see glossary, page 195)

salt

❶ Combine all the ingredients except the salt in a 6-quart stockpot. Add cold water to fill the pot three-fourths full. Slowly bring to a boil over medium heat, uncovered. Turn down the heat as low as possible and simmer, uncovered, for 3 hours. Spoon the foam occasionally. Add salt and taste for seasoning. ❷ Strain the stock through a colander or strainer lined with cheesecloth. Let it cool, then cover and refrigerate until the fat hardens on the surface. With a large spoon, remove the hardened fat from the surface and discard it, then use the stock as desired. ❸ If not using immediately, pour the stock into containers and refrigerate.

Advance Preparation: If not used within 3 days, the stock should be frozen and then reboiled before using. Freeze for up to 2 months.

[MAKES ABOUT 3 QUARTS]

roasted garlic purée

This is the simplest way to prepare this incredibly versatile flavoring agent. If you are able to find a market that sells individual peeled garlic cloves, it's even easier. Simply cut off the root end of the cloves and place the cloves in the foil as directed in the recipe. I like to roast about 20 cloves at a time. Once they are roasted, place them in a small container and mash them up.

❶ Preheat the oven to 425 degrees F. Using a sharp knife, cut off the top quarter of each head of garlic. Then score each head gently, cutting through a few layers of the papery skin all around the diameter. Pull off all the loose skin from the top half, trying not to remove every shred. (This will make it easier to squeeze out the cooked cloves later.) Sprinkle with a bit of olive oil. ❷ Wrap each garlic head tightly in a piece of aluminum foil. Place on a baking sheet and bake for 45 minutes to 1 hour, or until the garlic is soft when pierced with a knife. Remove from the oven and let cool. Using your fingers, squeeze the soft garlic pulp into a small bowl, then use as desired.

Advance Preparation: Can be prepared up to 3 days ahead, covered, and refrigerated.

[MAKES 2 TO 3 TABLESPOONS]

2 heads garlic
olive oil

herb vinaigrette

This vinaigrette is my standby salad dressing and can be varied according to whichever fresh herbs you have on hand. If you like the full-bodied flavor of balsamic vinegar, replace half of the red wine vinegar with balsamic. You can also add a tablespoon or two of nonfat plain yogurt for a creamier version.

1 shallot, finely chopped

1 garlic clove, minced

1 tablespoon finely chopped parsley

1 tablespoon finely chopped chives

1 teaspoon grainy mustard

1 tablespoon fresh lemon juice

3 tablespoons red wine vinegar

¾ cup olive oil

salt and freshly ground black pepper

❶ Combine the shallot, garlic, parsley, chives, mustard, lemon juice, and vinegar in a bowl and whisk until well blended. (Or place in a small food processor fitted with the metal blade and process until well blended.) ❷ Slowly pour the olive oil into the bowl, whisking (or processing) continuously until blended. Add the salt and pepper and taste for seasoning.

Advance Preparation: Can be prepared up to 1 week ahead, covered, and refrigerated. Bring to room temperature and whisk before using.

[MAKES ABOUT 1 CUP]

peeled peppers or chiles

Have you ever wondered why peeled peppers are called roasted peppers? I have, and still do. The fact is, peppers must be charred close to the heat so that the skin will blister and separate from the meat of the pepper. Roasting peppers in the oven will cook them too much. They should be grilled or broiled for best results. Make sure to select firm-fleshed, thick-skinned peppers so they will retain their texture. Sweet bell peppers, Anaheims, and poblanos work well with this method.

2 peppers

❶ Prepare a charcoal or gas grill for medium-high-heat grilling, or preheat a broiler. Place the peppers on a grill rack or a broiler pan and grill or broil about 3 inches from the heat, turning as necessary, until the skin is blistered and slightly charred on all sides. Always use long tongs to turn the peppers. Never pierce the peppers or the juices will escape.
❷ Put the peppers in a brown paper bag and close it tightly. Let the peppers rest for 10 minutes. Remove the peppers from the bag and drain off the accumulated juices. Peel off the charred skin with your fingers. Make a slit in each pepper and open it up. Cut out the core and stem, and scrape away the seeds and ribs. Cut the peppers with a sharp knife or a pizza cutter as desired.

Advance Preparation: Can be made up to 3 days ahead, covered, and refrigerated.

[MAKES 2 PEPPERS]

basic roasted beets

When working with beets, remember to wear rubber gloves and to place a sheet of waxed paper on the cutting board to avoid staining your hands or work surface red. Preparing beets by this method ensures that they will cook evenly. Use them diced in salads or even sautéed with a bit of orange zest and butter for a colorful side dish.

3 beets

❶ Preheat the oven to 425 degrees F. Trim and scrub the beets, but do not peel and be careful not to break the skin. Place them in a roasting pan and add water to a depth of ¼ inch. Cover the pan with foil, place in the oven and roast for 45 minutes, or until fork tender. ❷ Remove from the oven and, when cool enough to handle, use a small knife to remove the skins. Use as desired.

Advance Preparation: Can be made up to 3 days ahead, covered, and refrigerated.

[MAKES 3 BEETS]

Once an exotic condiment reserved for Italian cooking, pesto has become an American staple. The rich garlic-and-herb-flavored paste livens up pasta, pizza, soups, vegetables, and sauces. This classic version can be varied with different greens such as spinach or arugula.

❶ With the motor running, add the garlic cloves to a food processor fitted with the metal blade. Process until puréed. Add the basil and parsley and process until finely chopped. Add the pine nuts and finely chop. ❷ With the motor running, slowly pour in the olive oil in a fine stream. Add the pepper. ❸ Add the cheese and process until well blended. Taste for seasoning. Refrigerate the pesto in a tightly covered container until ready to use.

Advance Preparation: Can be prepared up to 1 week ahead through step 2, covered, and refrigerated. Add the cheese just before serving.

[MAKES ABOUT 1 ½ CUPS]

2 garlic cloves

2 cups medium-packed basil leaves
    (about 2 bunches)

½ cup parsley leaves

2 tablespoons pine nuts

½ cup olive oil

freshly ground black pepper

¾ cup freshly grated Parmesan cheese

sun-dried tomato pesto

The intense flavor of sun-dried tomatoes makes this versatile pesto ideal for spreading on Parmesan Crisps (page 26) or swirling into Lima Bean Soup with Sun-Dried Tomato Cream (page 35). As an alternative to oil-packed sun-dried tomatoes, place dry-packed sun-dried tomatoes in a heatproof bowl, add boiling water to cover, and let stand for about 30 minutes, or until softened. Drain and proceed with the recipe.

2 garlic cloves

½ cup oil-packed sun-dried tomatoes, drained (reserve oil) and chopped

2 tablespoons finely chopped fresh basil leaves

2 tablespoons freshly grated Parmesan cheese

1 tablespoon reserved oil from tomatoes or olive oil, or as needed

salt and freshly ground black pepper

❶ With the motor running, add the garlic cloves to a food processor fitted with the metal blade. Process until puréed. Add the tomatoes, basil, cheese, oil, salt, and pepper, and process until a thick paste forms. If it is too thick you may need to add a bit more oil. Refrigerate the pesto in a tightly covered container until ready to use.

Advance Preparation: Can be prepared up to 1 week ahead, covered, and stored in the refrigerator.

[MAKES ABOUT ½ CUP]

This rich tomato sauce is wonderful on pizzas, meat loaves, and pasta. Store in 1- or 2-cup containers in the freezer.

❶ Place the sun-dried tomatoes in a small bowl and pour boiling water over them. Let them steep for 5 minutes. Drain the slightly softened tomatoes and reserve. ❷ In a large nonaluminum Dutch oven or other heavy pot, heat the oil over medium heat. Add the onion, carrot, and celery, and cook, stirring frequently to avoid burning, for about 10 minutes, or until softened. Add all of the canned tomatoes, the softened sun-dried tomatoes, the garlic, wine, water, parsley, thyme, and basil. Cover partially and reduce the heat to medium-low. Simmer, stirring occasionally, for 1½ hours, or until the flavors are well blended and the sauce has thickened. Add the salt and pepper. ❸ Purée the mixture with a hand blender or in a food processor fitted with the metal blade until the sauce is a fine purée with no large pieces of tomato. You may need to add more water for a saucelike consistency since the sun-dried tomatoes provide extra thickness. Taste for seasoning. Serve hot.

Advance Preparation: Can be prepared up to 5 days ahead, covered, and refrigerated. It also can be frozen in small containers for up to 2 months. Reheat gently.

[MAKES ABOUT 2 QUARTS]

1 package (3-ounces) dry-packed
    sun-dried tomatoes (about 1 ¾ cups)
2 tablespoons olive oil
1 onion, finely chopped
1 carrot, peeled, finely chopped
1 stalk celery, finely chopped
1 can (28-ounces) crushed tomatoes
1 can (14-ounces) diced tomatoes
2 garlic cloves, minced
1 cup full-bodied red wine such as Chianti
    or Merlot
2 cups water
¼ cup finely chopped parsley
1 teaspoon finely chopped fresh thyme or
    ½ teaspoon dried
¼ cup finely chopped fresh basil or
    2 tablespoons dried
salt and freshly ground back pepper

red pepper–tomato sauce

This sauce is easy to prepare, and a wonderful alternative to traditional tomato sauces. Here, half of a chipotle chile has been added to deepen the flavor and add a hint of full-bodied heat. If you prefer a spicier sauce, go ahead and use a whole chile. Use canned chipotles packed in *adobo* sauce for the best flavor.

3 tablespoons olive oil

1 onion, finely chopped

4 large or 5 medium red bell peppers,
   seeded and thinly sliced

2 large tomatoes, peeled, seeded and finely
   chopped

½ canned chipotle en adobo, *coarsely*
   chopped

1 bunch fresh basil, coarsely chopped

salt and freshly ground black pepper

❶ In a large nonaluminum saucepan, heat the olive oil over medium heat. Add the onion and sauté for 3 to 5 minutes, or until softened. ❷ Add the bell peppers, tomatoes, chile, and basil, cover partially, and cook over medium-low heat for about 20 minutes, or until softened. Remove from the heat. ❸ Purée the vegetables in a food processor fitted with the metal blade for about 1 minute until the mixture is smooth with some texture remaining. Add the salt and pepper. Taste for seasoning.

Advance Preparation: Can be prepared up to 3 days ahead, covered, and refrigerated. Reheat gently. It may also be frozen up to 1 month.

[MAKES ABOUT 4 CUPS]

tomatillo salsa

This zesty Southwest-style sauce is equally good on your favorite eggs, as a marinade, or put out with a bowl of tortilla chips. If you can't find fresh tomatillos, substitute drained canned tomatillos with a pinch of sugar.

❶ In a large skillet, combine the stock and onion over medium heat. Cover and simmer about 5 minutes, or until softened. Add the tomatillos and continue to cook, covered, for another 5 minutes, or until the tomatillos are softened. ❷ Pour the tomatillo mixture into a food processor fitted with the metal blade and process until coarsely chopped. Add the garlic, cilantro, cumin, lemon juice, chile, salt, and pepper and process for 10 seconds. Taste for seasoning. Pour the salsa into a storage container and let cool. Refrigerate until ready to use.

Advance Preparation: Can be made up to 5 days ahead, covered, and refrigerated in an airtight container.

[MAKES ABOUT 2 ½ CUPS]

¾ cup chicken stock

1 small onion, finely diced

1 pound tomatillos, husked and quartered

2 garlic cloves, minced

3 tablespoons finely chopped cilantro

¼ teaspoon ground cumin

1 tablespoon fresh lemon juice

1 serrano chile, seeded, if desired, and chopped

salt and freshly ground black pepper

island salsa

Cooling tropical fruits pair up with cilantro, garlic, and red pepper flakes to make a sweet-and-spicy salsa. The fresh fruit and crunchy jicama create a colorful combination that livens up grilled fish, black beans, or quesadillas.

1 cup diced (¼-inch dice) fresh pineapple

1 mango, peeled and cut into ¼-inch dice

½ cup peeled and diced jicama
    (¼-inch dice)

1 tablespoon finely chopped cilantro

1 garlic clove, minced

¼ teaspoon crushed red pepper flakes

salt and freshly ground black pepper

❶ In a small bowl, combine all the ingredients and taste for seasoning. Cover and refrigerate until serving.

Advance Preparation: Can be made up to 1 day ahead, covered, and refrigerated.

[MAKES ABOUT 2 CUPS]

caramelized fennel and red onions

Microbreweries and mail-order beer companies are spreading across America, and beer is rapidly becoming an essential part of the country's cuisine. Much to the delight of the growing number of beer aficionados, Americans are discovering that unique brews complement the bold flavors of bistro cooking. A simple dish with complex flavors, this onion-and-fennel combination involves a beer reduction and is delicious served alone on crusty bread, as a bed for Grilled Veal Sausages with Sautéed Apples and Caramelized Fennel and Red Onions (page 98), or as a filling for Griddled Quesadillas with Caramelized Fennel and Red Onions (page 28). The flavor of the beer will intensify and affect the final taste of this relish, so use an ale that you enjoy drinking.

❶ In a large skillet heat the butter and olive oil over medium heat. Add the onions and fennel and cook, stirring often, for about 15 minutes, or until soft and golden brown. Sprinkle with sugar and continue to cook for another 5 to 7 minutes, or until dark brown and caramelized. ❷ Pour in the ale and simmer over medium heat for about 5 minutes, or until most of the liquid has evaporated and the vegetables are very soft. Add the salt and pepper and taste for seasoning.

1 tablespoon unsalted butter

1 tablespoon olive oil

2 large red onions, thinly sliced

2 fennel bulbs, trimmed and thinly sliced

1 teaspoon sugar

1 bottle (12-ounces) amber ale

salt and freshly ground black pepper

Advance Preparation: Can be prepared up to 3 days ahead, covered, and refrigerated. Remove from the refrigerator 1 hour before using.

[MAKES ABOUT 2½ CUPS]

cinnamon spice apple sauce

This all-American condiment uses honey instead of sugar for a slightly different flavor. Remember that the amount of sweetness depends on the sweetness of the apples, so take a bite before cooking. Combining the soft-textured McIntosh with the crisp pippin or Granny Smith apple results in a multitextured apple sauce. The apples are covered during the first stage of cooking, essentially steaming them, and then uncovered so that the liquid can reduce and intensify in flavor. I like to serve the apple sauce as a compote for brunch, with Crispy Potato Pancakes (page 135), or with Braised Brisket of Beef with Onions and Garlic (page 92).

3 McIntosh apples, peeled, cored, and cut into 2-inch chunks

3 pippin or Granny Smith apples, peeled, cored, and cut into 2-inch chunks

6 tablespoons honey

1 tablespoon ground cinnamon

1 tablespoon fresh lemon juice

❶ Place all the ingredients in a heavy nonaluminum saucepan over medium heat. Cover and simmer for about 12 minutes, or until the apples are slightly softened. ❷ Uncover and continue cooking , stirring occasionally to break up the large pieces, for 7 to 10 minutes, or until the apples are soft but there is still some texture. Adjust the seasoning with more honey, ground cinnamon, and/or lemon juice. Remove from the heat, let cool, and chill before serving.

Advance Preparation: Can be prepared up to 1 week ahead, covered, and refrigerated.

[MAKES ABOUT 4 CUPS]

The following menus are suited to a variety of occasions. You may find that certain recipes within a menu may yield a different number of servings. Consider adjusting a recipe in order to accommodate the number of guests you are planning on serving. In some cases you may have leftovers, which are often the best part of cooking for a crowd. The point is to be aware of creating the right balance for your menu, keeping in mind that it may be more appropriate to serve smaller portions when you have a large menu.

AMERICAN BISTRO CAESAR SALAD WITH ROASTED GARLIC DRESSING
GRILLED VEAL CHOPS WITH FRESH THYME
ROASTED SUMMER TOMATOES — Summer Menu
HERBED GARLIC CHEESE BREAD
PEACH AND PLUM CROSTATA WITH VANILLA ICE CREAM

BISTRO PÂTÉ WITH CORNICHONS, OLIVES, AND ASSORTED MUSTARDS
CHILLED HERBED CUCUMBER SOUP
SUMMER PICNIC SANDWICH — Summer Picnic Lunch
HEATH BAR CHOCOLATE CHIP COOKIES
ASSORTED SUMMER FRUITS (CHERRIES, APRICOTS, PEACHES, AND NECTARINES)

PARMESAN CRISPS WITH ROASTED EGGPLANT-GARLIC SPREAD
GOAT CHEESE—STUFFED HAMBURGERS WITH TWO-OLIVE SPREAD
GREEN BEAN, SWEET PEPPER, AND JICAMA SALAD — Summer Cookout
ORZO SALAD WITH TOMATOES, BASIL, AND FETA
ULTIMATE ICE CREAM SUNDAE

Early Fall Vegetarian Dinner ———— WILTED GREENS WITH GRILLED PORTOBELLO MUSHROOMS AND
DRIED CHERRY VINAIGRETTE
GARDEN VEGETABLE STEW WITH COUSCOUS <u>OR</u>
POLENTA LASAGNA WITH TOMATOES AND PEPPERS
PUMPKIN CARAMEL FLAN

Super Bowl Party ———— GRIDDLED QUESADILLAS WITH CARAMELIZED FENNEL AND RED ONIONS
TOMATILLO CHICKEN SALAD WITH CREAMY PUMPKIN SEED DRESSING
SOUTHWESTERN-STYLE BEEF CHILI <u>OR</u>
SPICY BLACK BEANS WITH ISLAND SALSA
HERBED GARLIC CHEESE BREAD
ULTIMATE ICE CREAM SUNDAE

Thanksgiving ———— SMOKED FISH MOUSSE
ROASTED BUTTERNUT SQUASH—SWEET POTATO SOUP WITH
HERBED SOUR CREAM
CHOPPED WINTER SALAD WITH LEMON-MINT DRESSING
SOY-AND-MOLASSES-BASTED TURKEY BREAST WITH
DRIED CRANBERRY—APPLE COMPOTE
PERFECT MASHED POTATOES
ROASTED SEASONAL VEGETABLES
PUMPKIN CARAMEL FLAN <u>OR</u> PUMPKIN ICE CREAM PIE
WITH GINGERSNAP CRUST
WINTER APPLE CRISP WITH DRIED FRUITS

WHITEFISH TERRINE WITH BEET-HORSERADISH RELISH
BRAISED BRISKET OF BEEF WITH ONIONS AND GARLIC
GARDEN VEGETABLE SAUTÉ
CRISPY POTATO PANCAKES
CINNAMON SPICE APPLESAUCE
CHOCOLATE CELEBRATION CAKE

Hanukkah Party

TUNA TARTARE WITH CUCUMBER-AVOCADO RELISH
PARMESAN CRISPS WITH TWO-OLIVE SPREAD AND
ROASTED EGGPLANT-GARLIC SPREAD
BELGIAN ENDIVE SPEARS WITH HERBED CREAM CHEESE
AND SMOKED SALMON
CRAB CAKES WITH CITRUS-MINT SALSA
CHICKEN BROCHETTES WITH ORANGE-HONEY-MUSTARD GLAZE (SEE PG. 81)
ROASTED PEARS IN RED WINE—CARAMEL SAUCE
HEATH BAR CHOCOLATE CHIP COOKIES

Holiday Cocktail Party

CRANBERRY-ORANGE SPARKLING WINE SPRITZERS
VEGETABLE FRITTATA
ROASTED NEW POTATOES WITH LEEKS
GRILLED ASSORTED BREAKFAST MEATS, SAUSAGES, BACON
STICKY BUNS OR APPLE SPICED STREUSEL COFFEE CAKE
CAPPUCCINOS

Fall Sunday Buffet Brunch

Quick Weekend Breakfast ----- FRESH GRAPEFRUIT

GRANOLA WITH MAPLE-YOGURT SWIRL

ORANGE JUICE OR TEA

Casual Dinner Party ----- LIMA BEAN SOUP WITH SUN-DRIED TOMATO CREAM

LEMON-ROSEMARY ROASTED CHICKEN

GARDEN VEGETABLE SAUTÉ

HERBED VEGETABLE RICE

MIXED BERRY BREAD PUDDING

New Year's Eve Party ----- CRISPY POTATO PANCAKES WITH CAVIAR

BELGIAN ENDIVE SPEARS WITH HERBED CREAM CHEESE AND SMOKED SALMON

MIXED GREENS WITH ROASTED BEETS AND TOASTED WALNUTS

GRILLED ENTRECÔTE

WHITE BEAN STEW WITH TOASTED BREAD CRUMBS

WARM CHOCOLATE PUDDING CAKES WITH VANILLA ICE CREAM

Seafood Celebration ----- BAKED ARTICHOKES WITH BREAD CRUMBS, SUN-DRIED TOMATOES, AND PARMESAN

CORNMEAL-CRUSTED SOFT-SHELL CRABS WITH LEMON-CAPER SAUCE

SHOESTRING POTATOES

FRESH FRUIT AND ASSORTED COOKIES

The following list of ingredients and techniques is intended to help you better understand certain foods and styles that are becoming increasingly popular in American restaurant and home kitchens. This array of domestic and foreign ingredients is an indispensable component of American bistro cooking.

Glossary

ancho chile: The dried form of the Poblano chile, this is the most commonly used dried chile in Mexico. Anchos are large and have a wrinkled appearance, a triangular shape, and a mahogany red color. This chile is moderately hot with fruity flavors and is available in Mexican specialty stores and supermarkets.

anchovy paste: Sold in a tube, anchovy paste is a combination of pounded anchovies, vinegar, spices, and water.

arborio rice: The key to making creamy risotto, Arborio is a variety of short-grain rice from Italy. Constant stirring while cooking helps to release the starch in the grains and create a creamy consistency. This rice is available in Italian markets and many supermarkets.

balsamic vinegar: Imported from Italy, true balsamic vinegar comes from only one region around the town of Modena in Emilia-Romagna. Balsamic vinegar is made by combining high-quality wine vinegar, reduced grape must (the partially fermented juice and pulp of the grape), some young balsamic vinegar as a starter, and sometimes caramel. Aging takes place in wooden casks of mulberry, juniper, and chestnut wood, and can take from a few years up to 120 years. It is a dark brownish red and is slightly thicker than the usual vinegar. For cooking, a commercial vinegar (versus the expensive artisan-produced vinegars) from Modena or nearby Reggio is fine. Check the label for either API MO (referring to Modena) or API RE (referring to Reggio) to be sure you aren't buying an imitation from another area. Look for a refined sweet-tart balance. If you find the vinegar is too strong and tart, reduce it by half over high heat to tame the acid and give it a syrupy consistency with a richer, more subtle flavor. Another way to balance the pungency is to add a pinch of brown sugar to each tablespoon.

black currant syrup: Black currants are tiny, round summer berries. They form the basis of the famous French liqueur crème de cassis, and are also used to make a thick, sweet, deep purple syrup that can be found at specialty- and natural-food stores.

blanching: To blanch means to cook a food briefly in boiling water and then cool the item by plunging it in cold water. This method is used with vegetables to set the color and cook them slightly, or to loosen the skins of tomatoes for easy peeling.

bouquet garni: This bundle of herbs is often used to flavor stocks. To make a bouquet garni, wrap a parsley stem, a bay leaf, and sprig of fresh thyme in cheesecloth and tie securely with a string. Tie the string to the handle of your pan to retrieve the bundle easily.

braising: A moist-heat cooking method used for meats and vegetables, braising means to cook, covered, in a small amount of liquid. Meats are usually browned first, and vegetables can be sautéed ahead of time, steps that give the foods a desirable texture and flavor prior to braising. Braising may be done on the stove top or in the oven.

chile paste: Used widely in Chinese cooking, chile pastes vary in degrees of hotness, flavor, and consistency. Most are made from fresh and dried chiles, vinegar, garlic, and seasonings, and a little goes a long way. Available in Asian markets and some well-stocked supermarkets.

chipotle chile: The smoked and dried version of the jalapeño, the chipotle is commonly available canned with garlic, tomatoes, and vinegar, labeled *chipotles en adobo*. The pepper is moderately hot and has a distinctive smoky flavor.

chocolate: American producers of chocolate traditionally relied on cocoa beans imported from tropical climates for domestic processing. Then, a few years ago, an entrepreneur discovered that the Hawaiian Islands were just as suitable for growing cocoa beans. Now Americans are both growing and producing chocolate, and Hawaiian Vintage Chocolate is considered to be among the best chocolate in the world (1-800-345-1543). Chocolate is sold in several forms. After the cocoa beans are roasted and ground, the resulting product is chocolate liquor, which contains cocoa butter. Cocoa is the dry powder that remains after part of the cocoa butter is removed from the chocolate liquor. Unsweetened chocolate is chocolate liquor with no added sugar, and is used in baking to flavor items that have other sources of sweetness. Bittersweet chocolate and semisweet chocolate are unsweetened chocolate with the addition of varying percentages of sugar and cocoa butter. Milk chocolate is sweetened chocolate to which milk solids have been added.

cider vinegar: Made from apple cider, this is the most common type of vinegar used for salad dressings and sauces and is available in supermarkets.

cilantro: Also known as fresh coriander or Chinese parsley, cilantro is often used in Asian and Latin American cooking. It has wide, flat leaves and a distinct flavor and aroma that liven up salads, salsas, and fish. Choose bright bunches of cilantro with fresh-looking leaves and stems.

coconut milk: Available canned or bottled in Asian markets and large supermarkets, coconut milk is made by combining equal parts water and shredded fresh coconut, simmering, and straining the milky liquid. Coconut milk is richly flavored, slightly sweet, and is widely used in Southeast Asian and Pacific cooking. Don't confuse this with the very sweet coconut milk mixes that are intended for mixed drinks.

couscous: A staple of North African cuisine, couscous is often referred to as a grain, but it is actually a type of pasta made from finely milled semolina wheat. Look for the quick-cooking variety that takes only 5 minutes. It is available in some supermarkets, Middle Eastern markets, and natural-food stores.

cracked wheat: Widely used in Middle Eastern and eastern Mediterranean cooking, cracked wheat has a nutty flavor and slightly crunchy texture. It can be used in pilafs, cereals, or salads. Cracked wheat can be found in supermarkets, natural-food stores, and Middle Eastern groceries.

cumin: This spice, with its distinct aroma, is used predominately in Mexican, Middle Eastern, and Indian cooking. It is available in the spice section of stores, either ground or in light brown seeds that can be toasted and ground. It should be used sparingly to enhance the flavors of meats and vegetables, not overwhelm them.

dark sesame oil: This rich, dark amber Asian oil tastes like toasted sesame seeds. It is used in small amounts to add a nutty flavor and aroma to dressings, marinades, and stir-fries. Do not confuse this sesame oil with the cold-pressed sesame-seed oil sold in natural-food stores.

demi-glace: *Demi-glace* is a concentrated brown liquid made by simmering veal or beef bones, vegetables, and seasonings together for hours. The thick, intensely flavored liquid is full of natural gelatin and is often used in sauces to accompany meats. You can make your own *demi-glace* or purchase it through gourmet shops. A company called More Than Gourmet ships containers of its Demi-Glace Gold nationwide (1-800-860-9392).

dried cranberries: Fresh cranberries grow wild in Massachusetts, Wisconsin, Washington, and Oregon, and are harvested between Labor Day and Halloween. Dried cranberries have a tart flavor and can be used like raisins in baking and cooking. Growing in popularity are sweetened dried cranberries (Craisins), which are slightly plumper and sweeter. Adjust your recipe in line with the sweetness of your dried cranberries.

european cucumber: This long, narrow, seedless cucumber is grown in hothouses. It is wrapped tightly in plastic and has a thin skin that does not require peeling. Keep the cucumber in its plastic wrapper in the refrigerator.

fennel: Sometimes called anise or finocchio, fennel is similar in appearance to a head of celery with a large bulb on the end and a faint licorice flavor. The stalk should be fresh, crisp, and solid, and the feathery leaves are excellent as garnish and for flavoring soups and salads. Cut off the stalks about 2 inches from the fennel bulb and use only the bulb in cooking.

feta cheese: Traditionally from Greece, feta is made from goat's or sheep's milk, and is cured in a salt brine. It is firm, tangy, and salty, although the saltiness often depends on the brand purchased. Feta is good in salads, dips, and as a garnish for pasta or vegetables.

flavored oils: Also called infused oils, these are made by steeping fresh herbs, fruits, vegetables, or spices in cooking oils. The results are highly aromatic and flavorful, and the oils can be used as ingredients or as condiments to drizzle over finished dishes. A variety of flavored oils made by Consorzio can be ordered from Napa Valley Kitchens (1-800-288-1089).

garlic: This popular seasoning has been grown in California since the 1920s. Before that it was imported to the United States from Italy. Today, Gilroy, California, is known as the Garlic Capital of the World. Fresh garlic is available year-round. It should be creamy white or have a purplish red cast, be plump and firm, and its paperlike covering attached snugly rather than shriveled. Store garlic in a cool, dry place with adequate ventilation (not in the refrigerator).

ginger: Fresh ginger, or gingerroot, is a knobby-looking rhizome with smooth, golden skin. Used regularly in Chinese and Japanese cooking, ginger has become a common ingredient in American cooking as well. It should be peeled first, then it can be shredded, grated, or cut into matchsticks. Do not substitute dried ginger for fresh.

goat cheese: Chèvre is French for "goat" and also for "goat cheese." Once only available imported from France, goat cheese is now produced by small cottage industries across the nation. The American version, which is slightly milder than European goat cheese, is generally sold fresh and has a soft texture, similar to cream cheese. It is good served warm on salad or as an ingredient in cold salads and pasta sauces. As goat cheese ages, it becomes stronger and its character becomes more pronounced.

grilling: A dry-heat method of cooking, grilling can be done on an open grid over charcoal, electric or gas elements, or in a grill pan. The cooking temperature is controlled by moving food to hotter or cooler places on the grill or pan.

hoisin: A deep reddish brown, sweet-and-spicy sauce used in Chinese cooking, hoisin, made from soybeans, vinegar, garlic, sugar, chile peppers, and spices, is thick and granular. It must be refrigerated once opened. Hoisin is available in jars in Asian markets and most supermarkets.

honey: Used as a sweetener long before sugar, honey comes in many types. They vary in flavor and appearance, ranging from thin to almost hard, and from white, golden, and amber to varnish-brown and even black. The most popular types are clover honey and orange honey, both of which are suitable for cooking and baking, but you can also find varieties such as lavender, sage, and wildflower at natural-food stores and farmers' markets. Honey helps retain moisture in baked goods, and can often be substituted for sugar in cooking. All honeys should be stored in tightly sealed containers, although eventually they will crystallize and harden with age.

horseradish cream: Horseradish grows in parts of Europe and the United States and is sold fresh in large, white, spicy roots for grating, or bottled. Bottled horseradish comes in white (preserved in vinegar) or red (in beet juice) and is found in the refrigerated section of supermarkets. Bottled horseradish cream is enriched with a touch of cream that smoothes out its strong pungent spiciness.

jack cheese: Often called Monterey Jack and produced on a large scale throughout the United States, Jack cheese is a mild, semisoft cheese with a high moisture content.

Jalapeño chile: This bright green, 1½-inch-long pepper ranges from hot to very hot and is one of the most widely used in the United States. It is available canned or fresh and is sometimes seen in its red ripe state. When working with chiles, always wear rubber gloves, and wash the cutting surface and knife immediately.

jicama: This root vegetable resembles a giant turnip and has a tan, leathery skin and sweet, white, crisp flesh. It is often used raw in salads or as a dipping vegetable. The tough skin must be peeled with a sharp paring knife before eating or cooking.

kalamata olive: These almond-shaped Greek olives are rich, salty, and slightly fruity in flavor. They are packed in a wine vinegar marinade and sold in jars with the pits intact or pitted.

lemon: One of the most versatile citrus fruits, the lemon has many culinary uses. A few drops of fresh lemon juice can enhance poultry, fish, vegetables, and baked dishes, and the acid can prevent fruits from turning brown when exposed to air. The peel is often grated and used as zest. Use only fresh lemon juice.

lime: Closely related to the lemon, the lime is sometimes used as a lemon substitute. The small, thin-skinned green fruit is used throughout the world, especially in juices, cocktails, preserves, salsas, and salads.

macadamia nuts: The buttery, rich macadamia nut is largely exported from Hawaii, but California cultivates the nuts as well. Since macadamias have a high fat content, they should be stored in the refrigerator once the jar or package is opened to prevent rancidity. Select the roasted and salted variety for cooking.

mango: Native to India, mangoes are also cultivated in the warm climates of Florida and California. Available May through September, the thin, tough skin is green and ripens to yellow with hints of red. Inside, the flesh is bright orange, juicy, sweet, and tart. The fruit must be carved from around the long, flat seed.

matzo meal: Unleavened bread called matzo is ground to make matzo meal. Traditionally eaten during the Jewish Passover holidays, matzo meal is available in Jewish markets and large supermarkets year-round.

mayonnaise: Considered a cold emulsified sauce, mayonnaise is essentially made from egg yolks, vinegar or lemon juice, seasonings, and oil. Commercial mayonnaise contains stabilizers to prevent the sauce from separating. Mayonnaise is often flavored with garlic to create aioli.

morel mushroom: Fresh wild morels are available in the spring months. Foraged in forests in the Pacific Northwest, Maryland, Virginia, Massachusetts, and Michigan, fresh morels possess a deep, earthy flavor. They have brownish spongelike caps and should be carefully cleaned by wiping with a damp soft brush or cloth. Dried morels may be substituted for fresh, but should be soaked in boiling water until hydrated.

mustard: Exotic mustards fill the shelves of American markets, but the most commonly used in cooking are the Dijon-style and grainy mustards. Dijon mustard is made by mixing ground mustard seeds, white wine, the sour juice of freshly squeezed green grapes, vinegar, and spices. Grainy mustards are of a more ancient origin and are coarser in texture. The hull of the mustard seed is retained and contains a strong enzyme that makes the flavor of the mustard more piquant.

olive oil: There are many types of olive oils, each possessing different characteristics based on the olive variety, the climate of the soil, and the amount of processing involved. Extra-virgin olive oils are cold pressed, rich, and full flavored. Pure olive oils, which have been heated and pressed to extract the last bit of oil, are milder in flavor. A cold-pressed extra-virgin olive oil is usually fruity, green, and redolent of olives. The cold-pressed oil is wonderful when used unheated in salad dressings or drizzled over vegetables or bread. It's better to use a lighter-style olive oil for cooked dishes, however, so as not to overwhelm their delicate flavors. California olive oils are becoming increasingly competitive with their Mediterranean counterparts as the industry continues to grow.

pancetta: Although it comes from the same cut as bacon, pancetta is salted, lightly spiced, and then cured, rather than smoked. It can be ordered cubed or sliced either thick or thin. American bacon may be substituted if necessary.

panko: Japanese-style bread crumbs that are larger and coarser than Western-style bread crumbs, panko are actually dried, toasted flakes. They are available in plastic bags in Asian markets and supermarkets.

parmesan cheese: The authentic Italian Parmigiano-Reggiano comes from an area of Emilia-Romagna, where it is strictly licensed and has been produced in much the same way for almost 700 years. The cheese should be straw yellow and have a crumbly, moist texture. Look for the words Parmigiano-Reggiano stamped on the rind. Store well wrapped in plastic wrap in the refrigerator for up to 3 weeks. If it becomes dry, wrap it in moist cheesecloth. Grate Parmesan as needed for the best flavor.

pepitas: Used in Mexican cooking, pepitas are raw, green pumpkin seeds. They are also available roasted and salted, and are sold in bags in Latin markets and large supermarkets. If you can't find the roasted variety, you can toast the raw pumpkin seeds yourself. Simply place the pepitas in a skillet over medium heat, and toss them for 2 to 3 minutes, or until lightly crisp. Salt them to taste

pine nuts: Also called piñons, pine nuts have a creamy color and a rich nutty taste when toasted. Those grown in the United States are smaller than their European or South American counterparts. Use pine nuts as soon as possible after purchasing, as they go stale faster than other nuts. Store them tightly sealed in a dry place.

pistachios: California is the second-largest producer of pistachio nuts in the world. The natural color of the shell is grayish white, but sometimes you'll find pistachios dyed red for cosmetic reasons. Inside, pistachios have a vivid green color. The shelled, unsalted pistachios are commonly used in recipes and are available in most supermarkets. If you can't find them shelled, you can do this yourself easily.

poblano chile: Ranging from 3 to 5 inches long with a very wide base, the dark green poblano (which is called ancho when dried) is commonly used for stuffing. Its hotness can range from mild to medium. When working with chiles, always wear rubber gloves, and wash the cutting surface and knife immediately.

polenta: The Italian term polenta is used for both a type of meal ground from sweet corn and for the cornmeal porridge dish made from it. The meal is sold in two basic forms. Traditional polenta has a coarse texture and requires at least 30 minutes of cooking with constant stirring. Instant (precooked) polenta has a finer texture and takes far less time.

porcino mushroom: Also called cèpes, porcini are pale brown, smooth, and have a woodsy flavor. In the United States, porcini are most commonly found dried, although fresh specimens can usually be found in late spring through early summer and again in early fall. Dried porcini should be soaked in boiling water to rehydrate.

port wine: A sweet, fortified wine with a high alcohol content (18 to 20 percent), port was first produced in Portugal. Today, ports range in quality from the most expensive vintage ports (grapes of a single vintage aged for many years), to the lowest grade ruby ports. In the middle are tawny ports, blends of grapes from several vintages that are aged in wood longer than the ruby ports.

portobello mushroom: Large, dark brown, cultivated mushrooms, the portobello is the mature form of the crimino (also spelled cremino), a variation of the white mushroom. Portobellos have flat, open caps that can be as large as 6 inches in diameter, with a dense, meaty texture. The woody stems should be removed.

quinoa: Although it is often referred to as a grain, quinoa is technically the seed of an annual herb. It comes from the Andes, where the Incas call it the "mother grain" because of its high nutritional value. Ounce for ounce, quinoa has as much protein as meat, and a single cup has as much calcium as a quart of milk. It needs to be washed before cooking to remove the natural bitter substance in its coating. Look for quinoa in the bulk section of natural-food stores.

radicchio: The most common variety of radicchio is shaped like a small cabbage with tender red leaves and white stalks and veins. Although radicchio is relatively expensive, a little goes a long way. Its slightly bitter taste stands up to flavorful dressings, yet it is best when mixed with other greens. The leaves are also excellent grilled. Radicchio is imported from Italy and is also grown in the United States.

rice vinegar: Chinese and Japanese rice vinegars are milder and sweeter than regular distilled vinegars. They range in color from clear or golden to amber, and are available, plain, seasoned, or sweetened with sugar. Asian markets and supermarkets sell rice vinegar in bottles that will keep for several months, although they lose their flavor and intensity over time.

ricotta cheese: Smooth and milky tasting, ricotta is fresh, unripened Italian cheese made from the whey of cow's milk or sheep's milk, depending on the regional version. A low-fat variety is often available.

roasting: To roast means to cook foods, uncovered, by surrounding them with hot, dry air in the oven, and it is used for meats, poultry, fish, vegetables, and even fruit. Meats and poultry are often roasted on a rack inside a roasting pan to allow for even circulation of the hot air around the food.

sautéing: Literally translated "to jump" in French, sauté means to cook quickly in a small amount of fat. The pan should be preheated with the fat before adding foods so that they sear quickly, and there should be plenty of room in the pan so that the foods aren't crowded and end up simmering in their own juices.

serrano chile: Just over 1 inch long and very slender, serranos pack a lot of punch for their size. The bright green chiles turn red as they ripen and are very hot. When working with chiles, always wear rubber gloves, and wash the cutting surface and knife immediately.

shiitake mushroom: Dark brown shiitake mushrooms, common to Japanese and Chinese cuisines, are available fresh almost year-round. They have tan undersides, a rich, meaty texture, and a wild mushroom flavor. Dried shiitakes are available as well: soak them in water before using, and cut off the hard, knobby stem end. The soaking liquid can be strained and used to flavor soups and sauces.

sun-dried tomato: Drying tomatoes greatly intensifies their flavor and gives them a chewy texture. The southern Italians are masters of drying tomatoes in the sun: the plump meaty plum tomato is reduced to a leathery state, covered with olive oil and bottled. Dried tomatoes are now produced in America as well, and are available dry-packed or oil-packed. The latter can be halved or chopped. To rehydrate dried tomatoes, soak in boiling water for at least 20 minutes.

tomatillo: Resembling small green tomatoes, tomatillos are tightly covered in a thin tan husk that needs to be removed before using. Use tomatillos while they are still green and firm. Popular in the cuisines of Mexico and the Southwest, tomatillos are available in Latin markets and well-stocked supermarkets.

vanilla bean: Long, thin pods that should be flexible and aromatic when purchased, vanilla beans come from many parts of the world. The beans from Madagascar and Tahiti are considered the best, although the Tahitian beans are scarcer and more expensive. Vanilla beans are used to infuse flavor into a dish, and are usually removed at the end of the recipe. The bean should be split open lengthwise to release its full flavor. The used beans can then be rinsed, dried, and stored in sugar to create vanilla-flavored sugar for baking.

wasabi: The Japanese version of horseradish, wasabi comes from the root of an Asian plant and is one of the strongest spices used in Japanese cooking. It is sold fresh for grating, but is more commonly used in the paste or powder form. The powder is blended with water to make a thick, creamy paste. The pale green paste is fiery hot, so it should be used sparingly.

wild rice: Not really a rice, wild rice is the seed of an aquatic grass that has a taste similar to that of rice but is distinguished by a rich, nutty flavor. Originally only grown in Wisconsin and Minnesota, where water is plentiful for cultivation, wild rice is now grown in Northern California as well. The grains are long, slender, hard, and dark brown. Wild rice should be washed before using, and can be served alone or mixed with white rice.

Index

Table of Equivalents

The exact equivalents in the following tables have been rounded for convenience.

ABBREVIATIONS

US/UK

oz=ounce
lb=pound
in=inch
ft=foot
tbl=tablespoon
fl oz=fluid ounce
qt=quart

METRIC

g=gram
kg=kilogram
mm=millimeter
cm=centimeter
ml=milliliter
l=liter

LIQUIDS

US	METRIC	UK
2 tbl	30 ml	1 fl oz
¼ cup	60 ml	2 fl oz
⅓ cup	80 ml	3 fl oz
½ cup	125 ml	4 fl oz
⅔ cup	160 ml	5 fl oz
¾ cup	180 ml	6 fl oz
1 cup	250 ml	8 fl oz
1½ cups	375 ml	12 fl oz
2 cups	500 ml	16 fl oz

WEIGHTS

US/UK	METRIC
1 oz	30 g
2 oz	60 g
3 oz	90 g
4 oz (¼ lb)	125 g
5 oz (⅓ lb)	155 g
6 oz	185 g
7 oz	220 g
8 oz (½ lb)	250 g
10 oz	315 g
12 oz (¾ lb)	375 g
14 oz	440 g
16 oz (1 lb)	500 g
1½ lbs	750 g
2 lbs	1 kg
3 lbs	1.5 kg

LENGTH MEASURES

⅛ in	3 mm
¼ in	6 mm
½ in	12 mm
1 in	2.5 cm
2 in	5 cm
3 in	7.5 cm
4 in	10 cm
5 in	13 cm
6 in	15 cm
7 in	18 cm
8 in	20 cm
9 in	23 cm
10 in	25 cm
11 in	28 cm
12 in/1 ft	30 cm

OVEN TEMPERATURES

FAHRENHEIT	CELSIUS	GAS
250	120	½
275	140	1
300	150	2
325	160	3
350	180	4
375	190	5
400	200	6
425	220	7
450	230	8
475	240	9
500	260	10